ECHOES IN THE ABYSS

Cassandra Valentino

To all those who had the courage to love in the darkness of the night.

ENTRY POINT

Writing and drawing in my studio is an inexhaustible source of serenity for me.

Sunlight streams through a large window, flooding the space with a natural brilliance that awakens my creativity.

A delicate curtain adorned with a graphic element sways gently with every faint breeze, creating an intimate and welcoming atmosphere.

This stylized decoration reflects my deep connection with nature.

I love living in harmony with nature and never miss an opportunity to escape the city, far from the noise, accompanied only by my pen and notebook to capture and record every emotion.

The tranquility and beauty of natural settings constantly inspire me with new ideas and impressions.

Walking along the s horeline, listening t o the sound of waves breaking on the beach, or exploring trails through woods and meadows allows me to enter a state of inner peace and profound harmony with the universe.

My mind sheds the distractions of daily life, and I immerse myself entirely in my inner world.

Every landscape, every tree, every wave becomes a source of inspiration for my drawings and poems.

Sitting on a rock overlooking the sea or lying in the grass in an open field, I let nature speak to me, translating its voices and silences into drawn lines and written words.

Next to the window stands my desk, elegant and minimalist, made of smoky glass.

It is here that my creativity takes shape.

The desk is rarely tidy, often delightfully chaotic.

Scattered across its surface are various books on art and poetry, surrounded by bottles of ink, brushes, and markers, as well as my digital devices—essential tools for my creative work.

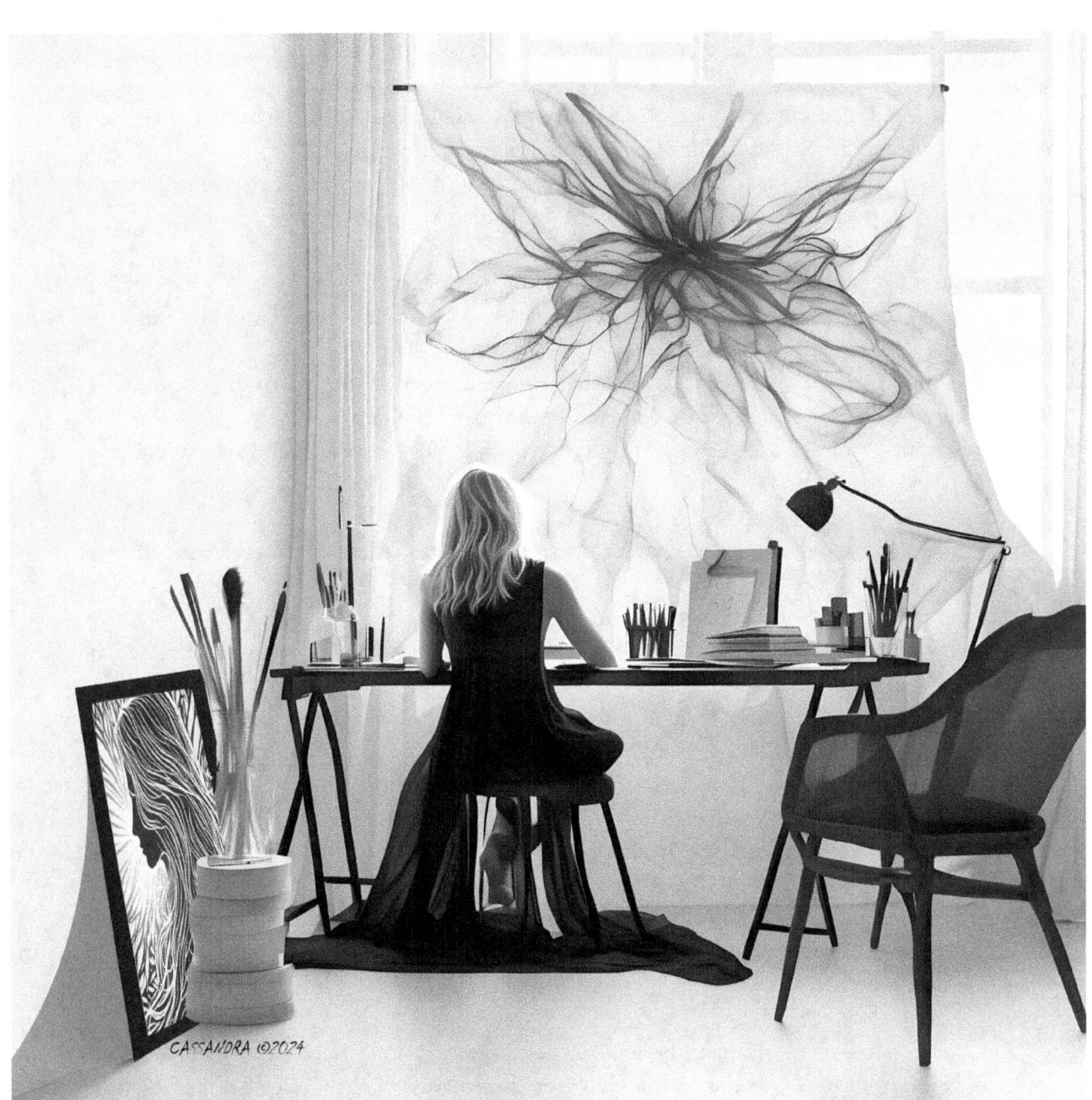

CASSANDRA ©2024

The front wall of my studio is the true visual focal point of the space, a dynamic mosaic of frames containing paintings, reproductions, and photographs.

Each displayed work is carefully selected and arranged with the intent of creating a stimulating and ever-evolving environment.

The variety of images, from natural landscapes to portraits, from botanical illustrations to abstract drawings, reflects my passion for art and nature, as well as my curiosity towards different styles and themes.

This wall is a reflection of my emotions and moods: I often change the arrangement of the works, highlighting different colors and illustrations depending on the moment.

Sometimes a particular piece captures my attention and becomes the focus point of the room; other times, I prefer a more understated arrangement that allows me to keep my mind clear.

The side walls, on the other hand, are intentionally left bare.

This open space represents a sort of mental blank canvas, a place where my ideas can flow without restrictions.

Their simplicity creates a contrast that balances the visual richness of the front wall, fostering concentration and offering a sense of peace and infinite possibilities.

In these empty walls, I see the opportunity to imagine new scenarios and let myself be inspired by what has yet to take shape.

Next to the drawings and photographs on the front wall, there are my books, arranged on thin shelves.

A special place on the shelves is reserved for my collection of vinyl records.

I love vinyl records not only for the covers, which are often works of art in themselves, but also for their analog sound, rich and nostalgic.

Music is a constant presence in my studio, a soundtrack that accompanies each of my creations.

From classical melodies that foster reflection, to modern rhythms that ignite inspiration, to new age sounds that instill calm, every note helps create the perfect environment for the creative process.

The plants, scattered across the shelves and on the floor, add a touch of green and life to my studio.

Their presence not only purifies the air but also brings a sense of tranquility and harmony.

Their forms and colors, so natural and organic, often influence my illustrations, bringing natural design elements into my works.

My studio is much more than just a workspace; it is a place where every element—from natural light to plants, from music to the seemingly casual but meticulously studied arrangement of tools—is designed to fuel my imagination and transform my visions into reality.

Every brushstroke, every ink stroke, every word written here reflects my essence and my passion for art

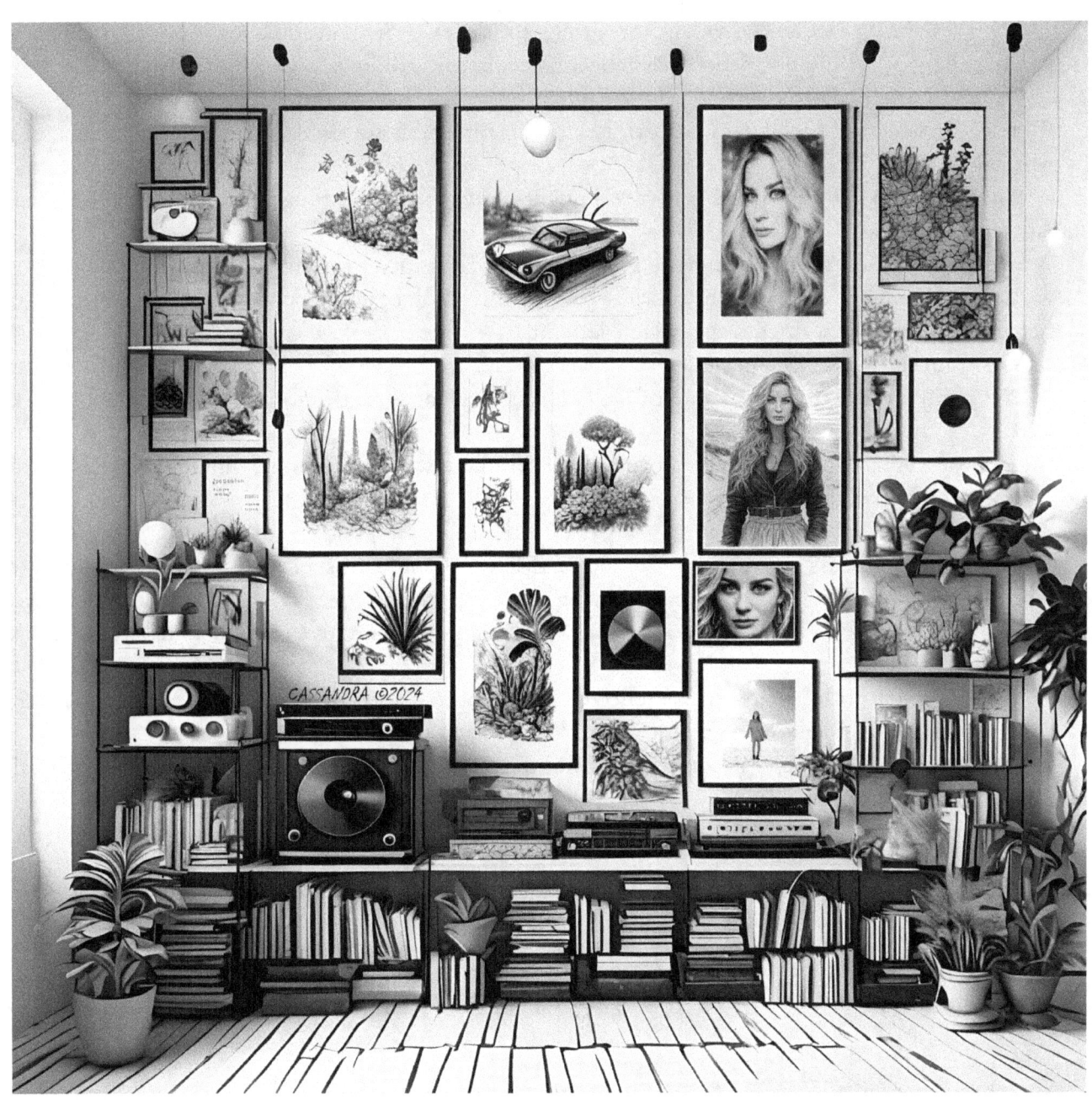

Art is an endless cycle, a perpetual dance between light and shadow, between highs and lows.

Each of my works is a step in this infinite journey, a path that inevitably returns to the starting point, marking my continuous evolution.

And every time I begin a new project, I embark on a familiar yet ever-new path, where every past experience contributes to shaping my current vision.

This cyclical process allows me to grow, to develop new techniques, and to deepen my understanding of art and life, which inevitably reflects in my creations.

Each drawing and each poem bear witness to this profound connection between my being and my expression.

My experiences, my emotions and my thoughts are expressed through art, becoming an integral part of my drawings

Every ink stroke, every written word is a reflection of my soul, a way to share my inner world.

Every movement, every brushstroke, is part of this choreography, an interplay of contrasts that merge and separate in a rhythm that will never end.

Music, music, music, the musicality of situations...

This cycle mirrors the very nature of life, with its challenges and victories, its moments of joy and sorrow.

It is through this dance that I explore and understand the world around me, finding balance between the opposites that define existence.

The creative process for me is a journey of discovery and introspection, aimed at exploring the depths of my imagination and emotions, seeking to capture the complexity of the human experience.

Each of my works is an attempt to create a visual and poetic narrative that resonates with the viewer and reader.

My connection with the universe is reflected in my approach to art, where every creation is part of a larger whole, a fragment of an endless story.

And every time I create, I become part of this universal web, contributing my small but significant voice to the chorus of humanity.

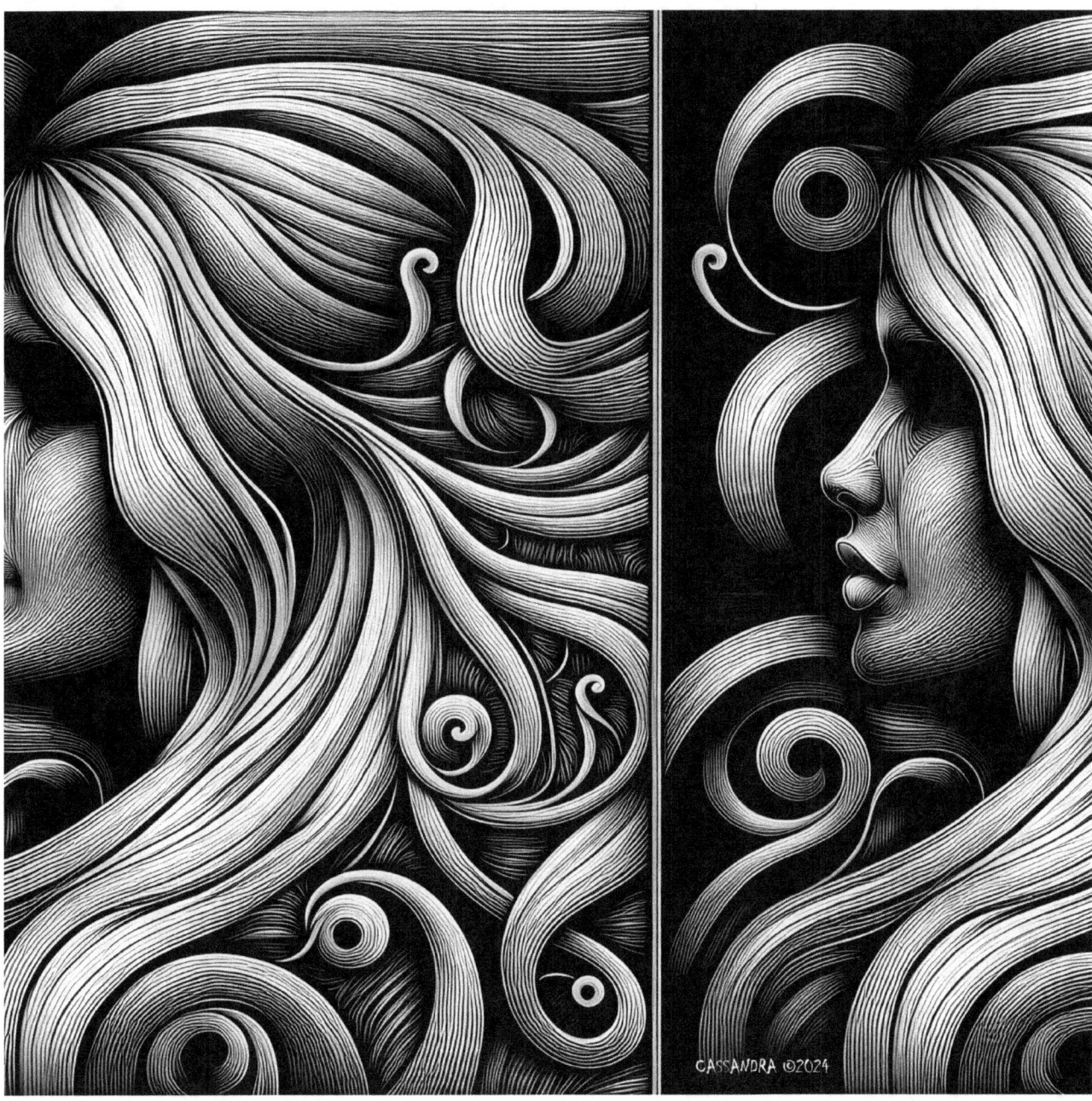

CASSANDRA ©2024

My artistic evolution is marked by a constant search for new forms of expression and new ways of understanding the world.

Each creation is a step forward on this path, a milestone in my personal and professional development.

This continuous growth is what makes art vital, a field where there is no definitive destination, only successive stages in an endless journey.

Through each drawing and each poem, I can express what words alone cannot explain, capturing the essence of my emotions and experiences.

This process of creation is both personal and universal, a way to connect with others and with myself.

And in every stroke, in every word, there is a fragment of my soul, an echo of my existence that resonates through time and space.

For me, the true joy lies in the act of creation itself, in watching the ink come to life on the paper.

Every line, every shade, every word is an experience that deeply connects me to my inner being.

It is a process that goes beyond mere technique: it is an emotional journey that transforms a blank page into a visual testimony of my most intimate feelings.

The love for art is part of me, an impulse I cannot ignore, a force that guides and motivates me every day.

A deeply instinctive approach allows me to be free in my expression, to let the art flow naturally without the constraints of a predetermined plan.

And often, I find myself completely immersed in the work, physically feeling what I am creating, as if the ink on the paper were coming to life before my eyes.

This state of total immersion is almost meditative, a kind of creative trance where time seems to stop and all that exists is the dialogue between me and my work.

Every word is a direct manifestation of my emotions and thoughts, every mark is a visual translation of my inner world.

The magic of the creative process lies in its unpredictability and its ability to surprise.

Every time I start a new project, I don't know exactly where it will lead me, but it is this very uncertainty that makes the journey so fascinating.

Art is not just the final result but the entire journey that leads me to that result.

It is a continuous exploration, an adventure that allows me to constantly discover something new about myself and the world around me.

This act of creation is as much physical as it is spiritual, an experience that engages mind, body, and soul.

My art is a reflection of my deepest essence, an instinctive and emotional expression that comes to life through ink on paper.

Each work is a part of me, a fragment of my artistic journey that continues to evolve with every new creation

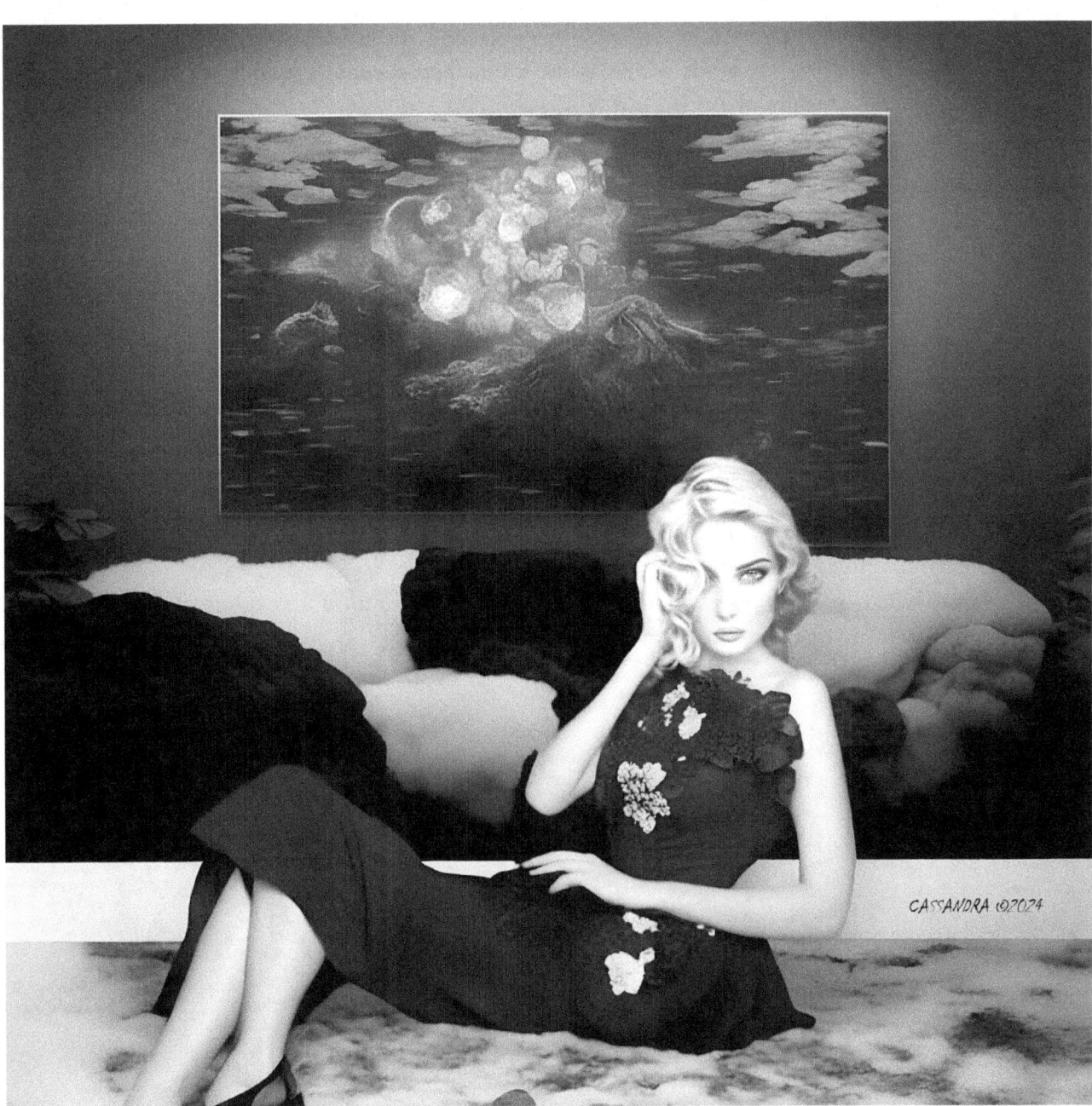

For the creation of the illustrations in *Echoes in the Abyss* I chose to work exclusively with black ink, occasionally diluted with water to produce a spectrum of gray tones.

Using brushes or markers, I bring to life the lines, shades, and nuances that animate my visions on pristine white sheets.

Some illustrations are crafted using a digital process on photographs of myself, infusing them with an aesthetic and symbolic dimension intricately connected to the book's themes.

This approach enriches my work, adding a fresh visual perspective that delves into the relationship between reality and interpretation.

Transforming a simple photograph or sheet of paper into a vibrant work of art allows me to immerse myself in a process that reflects my personal worldview.

Thus, my studio becomes a portal to fantastical realms and epic adventures, where every brushstroke or digital intervention gives birth to ethereal landscapes and dynamic figures.

My illustrations serve as the medium through which I explore the depths of my imagination.

Each of my pieces portrays a clear and precise image, without necessarily conveying an explicit message.

Its strength lies in the ability to evoke emotions and ignite the imagination.

The interplay of light and shadow, combined with the contrast of tones, contributes to a powerful visual impact that transcends mere drawing.

Figurative art represents for me a constant pursuit, an evolutionary process reflecting my state of mind and lived experiences.

Each work becomes an open window into my soul, an invitation to explore the worlds I create and to be swept away by the magic of my illustrations.

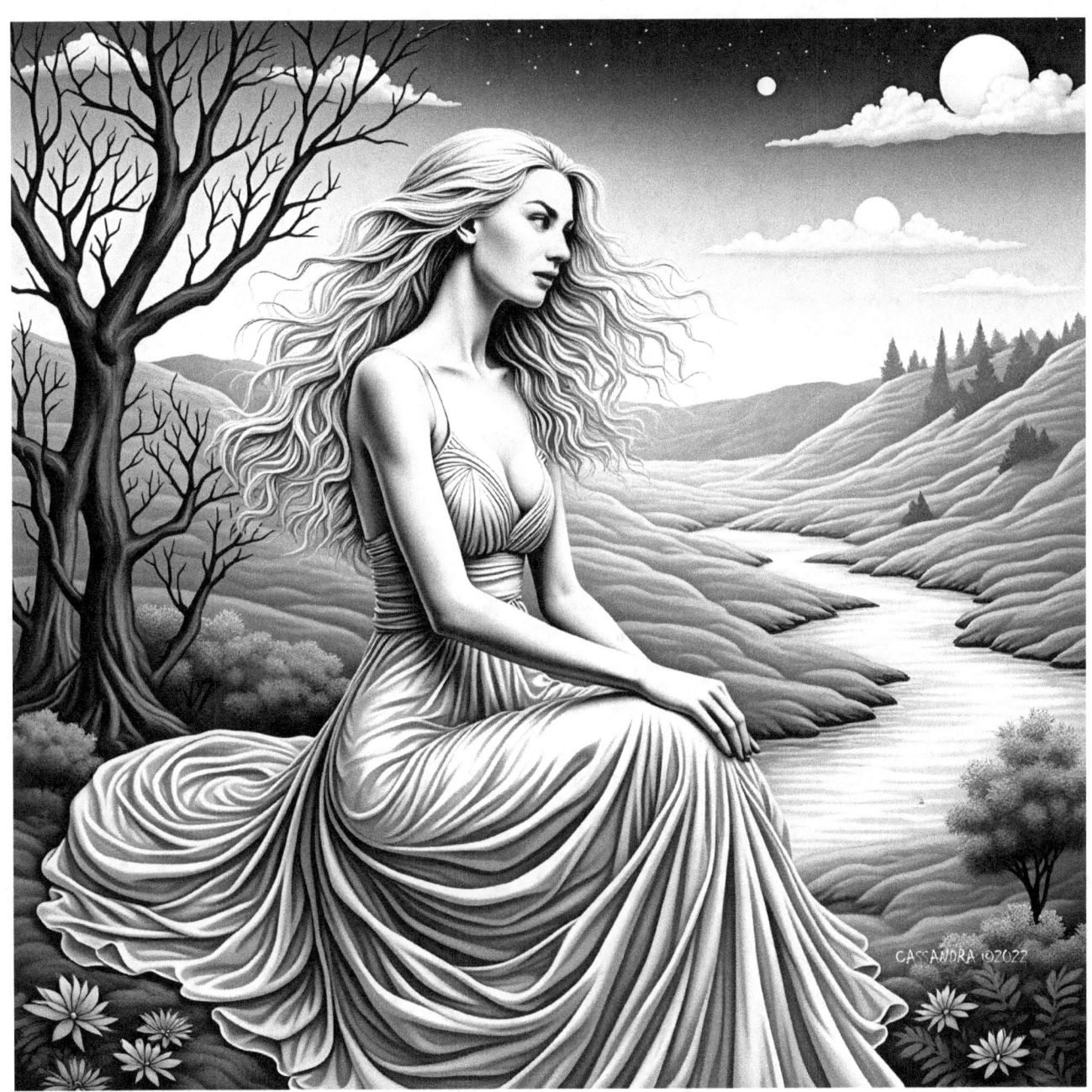

CASSANDRA ©2022

Each of my creations reflects my personal journey; it is an echo of my deepest experiences and the moments I have lived with intensity. In the same way, my poetic compositions emerge from a process of discovery and introspection.

To me, poetry is the art of capturing the essence of the soul and expressing inner turmoil through words that resonate with sincerity and depth.

Echoes in the Abyss is the result of my need to give voice to the darkest thoughts and deepest emotions.

I admire how they were able to capture the complexity of human feelings through words that resonate with the same frequency as the images I draw.

However, I want to clarify that writing, for me, is an art that goes beyond the simple word.

Writing is a medium through which I explore the depths of my soul and share my life experiences with the world.

My verses are not mere expressions of feelings, but each composition becomes a small universe of emotions and thoughts.

Although the writing process is deeply personal and reflective, the evocative metaphors in my poems aim to convey the complexity of human experiences.

Writing is, for me, a cathartic act: every word chosen, every verse composed is a fragment of my personal journey, an echo of my existence.

It is an act of transformation, where emotions crystallize into sounds that express truth and authenticity.

Through writing, I explore universal themes such as love, loss, hope, despair. I examine the human experience in the constant alternation of joys and sorrows, falls and recoveries, moments of light and shadow.

By witnessing my struggles and victories, I seek to establish a deep connection with the reader.

Each verse is an invitation to explore one's inner world, to find resonance, and to discover new perspectives of one's own existence through the reflection of my lived Life.

In conclusion, my poetry is an inner journey, a way to explore and understand myself and the world around me.

In my compositions, I try to give form to my experiences, transforming them into something universal and shareable.

Every work becomes a piece of the puzzle that composes my art, a step in this journey called LIFE.

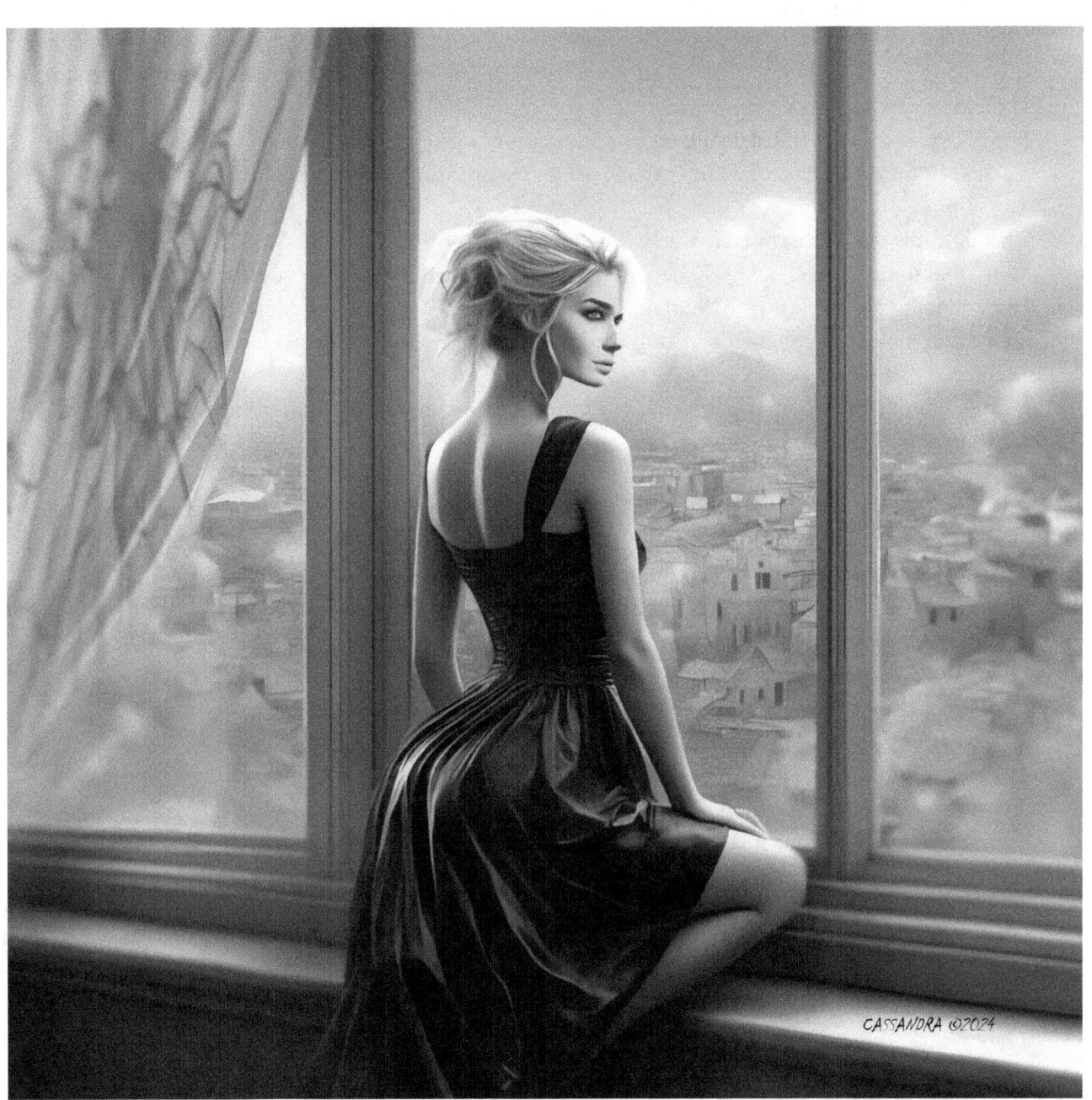

CASSANDRA ©2024

My work as a model is another fundamental expression of my art.

Posing makes me feel as if I were a canvas, a blank sheet ready to be sketched, like one and millions of pixels that the camera sensor disassembles and reassembles, capturing not only the shapes of my skin but also the lights and shadows of my soul.

Each pose is a brushstroke, ink that comes to life on the page.

Each pixel contributes to creating an image that tells stories of beauty, strength, and vulnerability.

My body becomes a living work of art, a medium that transforms every session into an experience of collaboration and discovery.

Every expression is carefully studied to convey an emotion, to tell a story.

Each shot becomes part of a larger work of art, contributing to the visual narrative of the artist.

Through this role, I discovered a new dimension of art.

When I assume a pose, my body becomes an integral part of the creative process.

Experiencing the power of the human form as an expressive tool has allowed me to see beauty from a different perspective, recognizing the strength of the body image as a means of artistic resonance.

Being a model has taught me to value every detail of my body and soul, transforming each performance into a shared creative journey.

In *Echoes in the Abyss* I chose to use myself as the main subject for my illustrations, assuming the dual role of model and artist.

This approach allowed me to explore my image from a unique perspective.

To create the illustrations, I was inspired by the poses I experimented with during my sessions, translating them into visual art.

Participating as a runway model adds further depth to my artistic experience.

Wearing designer clothes allows me to explore fashion as an art form.

Walking the runway is an exhilarating experience: my body becomes a medium to express the ideas and visions of designers, turning each garment into a living story.

The preparation, adrenaline, and the performance itself are moments of intense creativity and self-expression.

Fashion shows offer me the opportunity to interact with the work of designers, appreciating the details, structure, and innovation each piece brings.

These events not only enrich my experience as a model but also fuel my inspiration as a visual artist.

The textures, colors, and shapes of the clothes I wear often influence my illustrations, introducing new design elements into my work.

Exploring the beauty and strength of the body image has enriched me as an artist, allowing me to experience art not only as a creator but also as a muse.

This role has taught me to see my body as a powerful tool of expression, capable of conveying emotions and telling stories through every pose.

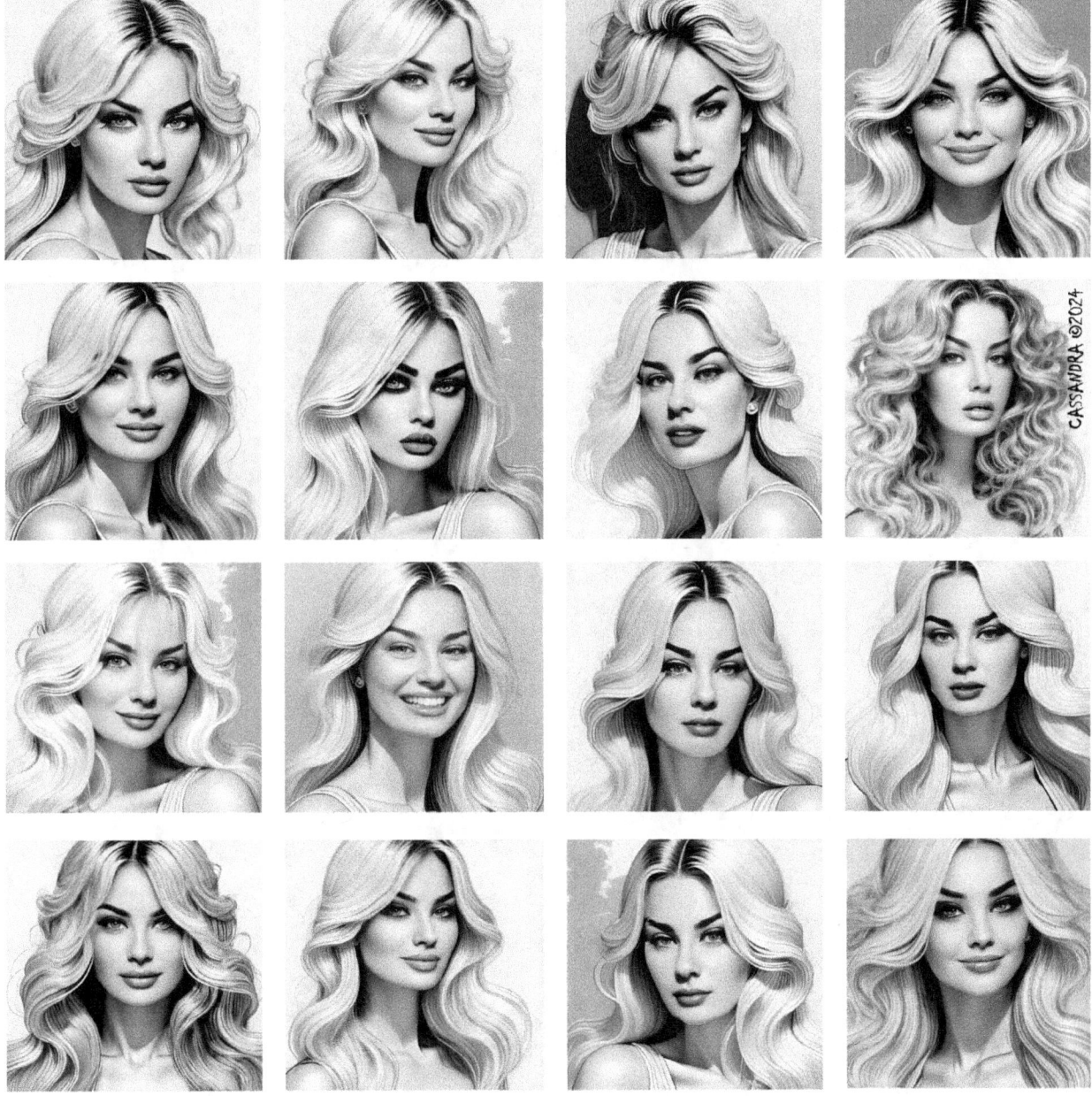

Through *Echoes in the Abyss*, I wish to convey not only my thoughts and feelings, but also offer you a space in which you can recognize yourself.

Although the experiences narrated are universal, ready to resonate within each of you, every poem and every illustration is a fragment of my lived life.

The creative process of this book has been a deep and transformative journey for me.

In the verses and illustrations, I have tried to shape my experiences, transfiguring them into something universal and shareable.

Each composition represents a step in this path.

I invite you to immerse yourself in these pages, to discover the emotions I wanted to share, and to find understanding in the words and illustrations.

I hope you will discover a reflection of your own experiences, and that my journey may, in some way, become yours as well.

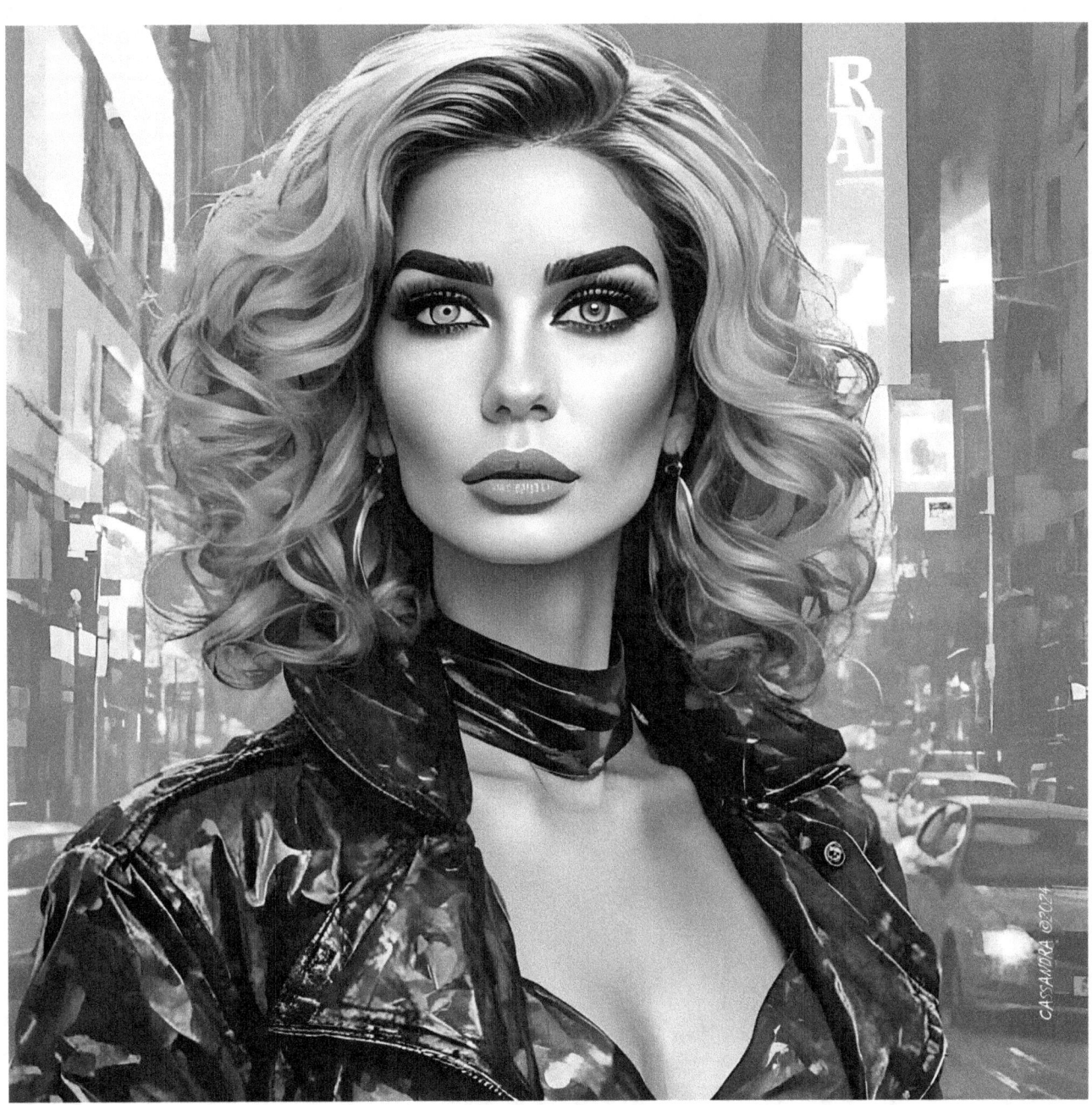

ECHOES IN THE ABYSS

In the shadows of this room,
where your breath entwines with mine,
I dissolve into the reflections of your skin.
I wish the wind could sweep away my thoughts,
yet they linger here, tethered to every moment of you.

My lips graze the silence
filling the distance between us.

I am like a breath of life, suspended,
a fleeting fragility turned eternal.

I gaze at you without seeing,
yet feel your eyes sinking into the folds
of my weary soul.

And you, unaware, claim my essence,
leaving me empty, yet brimming with longing.

I wonder where I end and you begin,
in the delicate weave of this melancholy that enfolds us.

If only I could speak to you with my hands,
tell you with a touch all that words cannot express...

But I remain here, with parted lips
you would have on you,
as I dream of your heart beating within my chest.

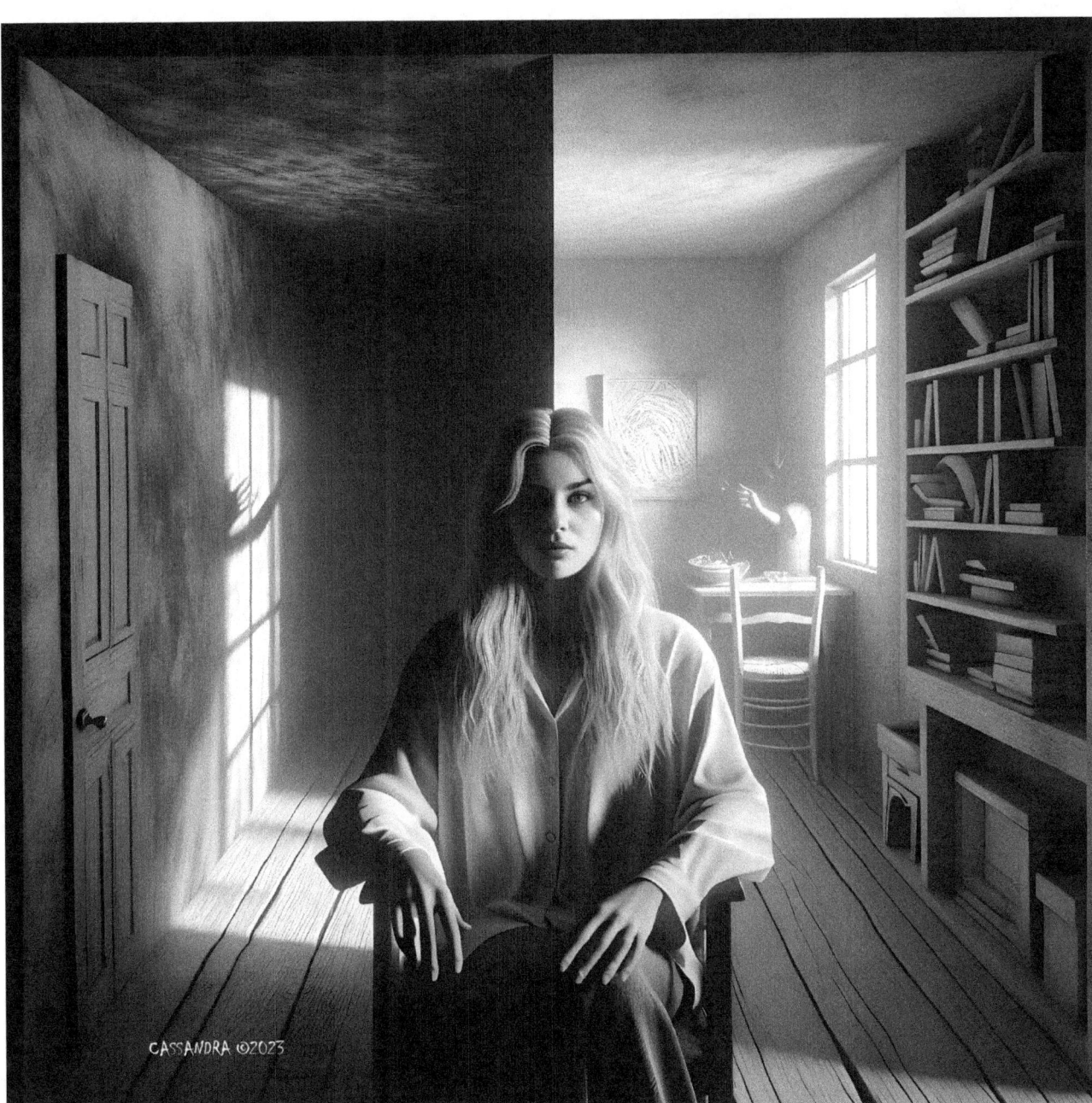

CASSANDRA ©2023

Between the echoes of reality
and the sinuous deceit,
delicate threads of truth and lies unravel,
dancing
in labyrinths of melancholy.

I believed, time and again, that it was true love,
when his sweet words wrapped me like silk
and his promises made me feel secure,
but pain, like shattering ice,
now tears through my heart.

In the bitter weeping of my betrayed soul,
I fiercely reject the falsehood,
unyielding,
invoking truth as a radiant flame
to pierce the darkness with its blinding light.

I wish to sing soft songs of forgiveness,
to recall the moments when our laughter filled the room
and offer clemency and compassion,
but pride bars the doors of his heart,
rejecting every offer of peace and redemption.

So I find myself surrounded by regrets,
not awaiting a dawn to bring liberation,
but realizing that only my inner fire
can dissolve the deception,
like dew under the first light of morning,
and transform my melancholy into strength and brilliance.

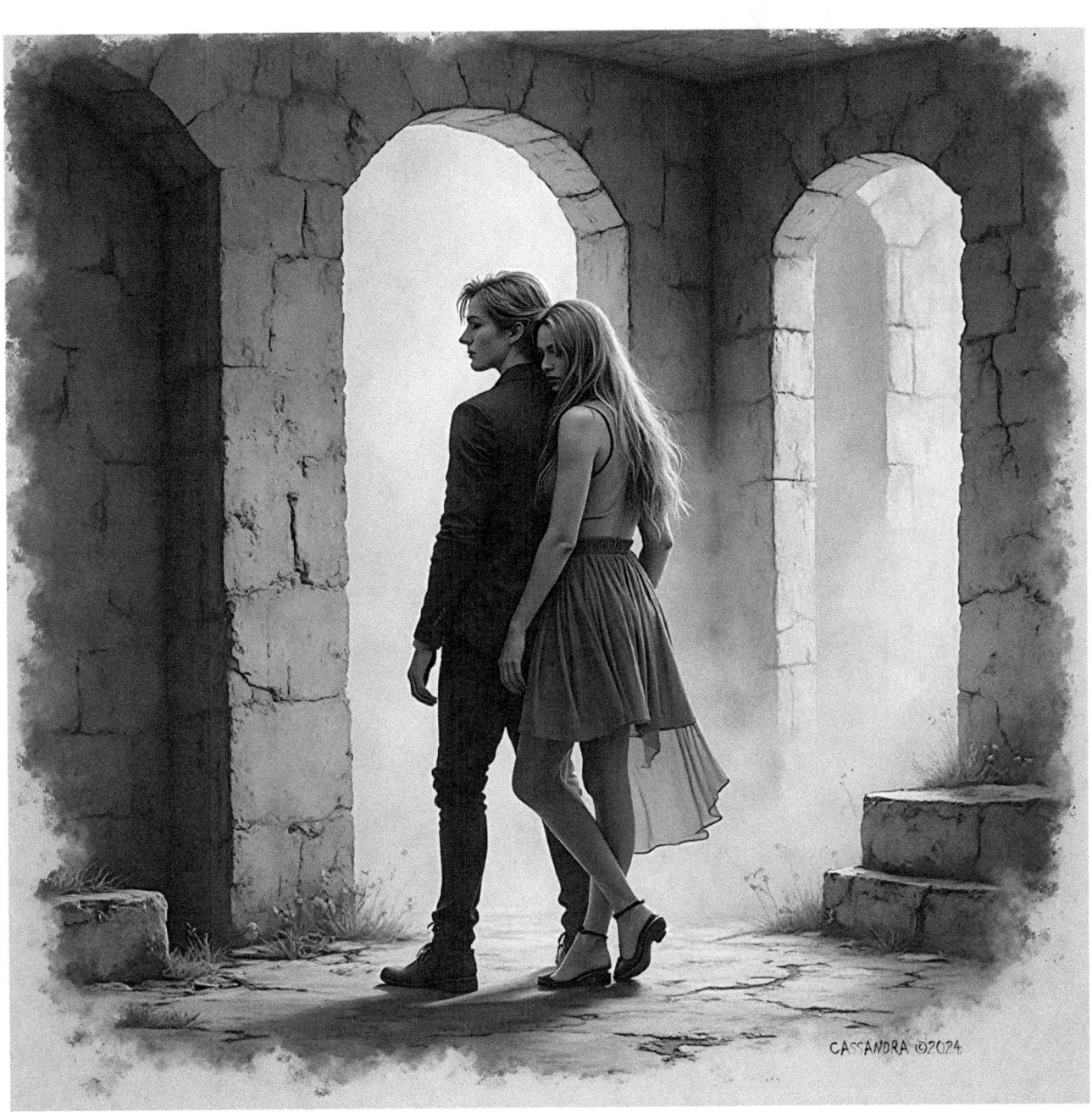

Through my hair slips
the weight of unspoken dreams,
like lights shattering
at the edges of the sky.

I am not the reflection
of any glow,
but the deep echo
of an abyss that calls to me.

My lips, silent,
tell stories unseen,
beneath this shroud of extinguished stars
where my heart walks barefoot.

I do not wish to burn
for a light that beguiles me,
nor to shine
with a brilliance that is not my own.

I am a soul made of shadows,
of truths buried beneath silence,
distant from the deceit of mirrors
that drape lies in gold.

In the darkness, I ignite,
and all that I am
is revealed in a whisper of flame.

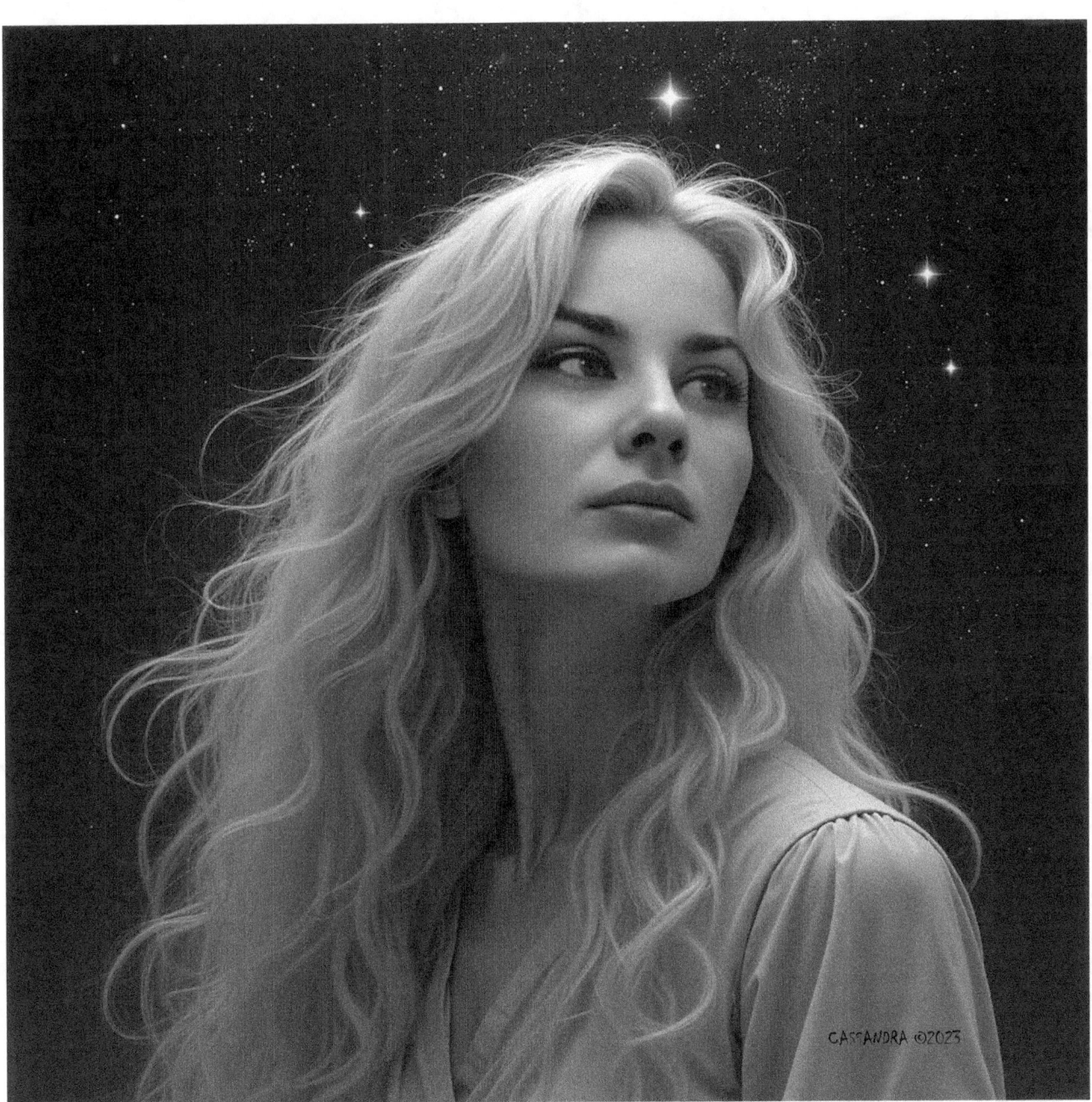

In the heart of a forgotten city,
I move through alleys damp with silence.
I wear the shadow of myself,
like a leather jacket that no longer warms.

My eyes reflect extinguished lights,
the neon tangles with the questions
that have followed me all my life.

I walk, lost yet present,
an echo of steps that never answers back.

The night grows heavier,
enveloping me like the embrace
of a past that won't let me go,
whispering secrets
I do not wish to hear.

An abyss follows me,
clinging like a desperate lover,
murmuring promises of eternity.

I meet its gaze
but cannot recognize it;
it is within me, outside me, everywhere,
and yet untouchable.

I am the woman
of this starless night,
bare skin beneath the rain
that blurs into the streets,
into weary lampposts.

And as the darkness grows inside,
I feel there are no answers to my questions.

Only this endless walking,
this abyss that calls my name.

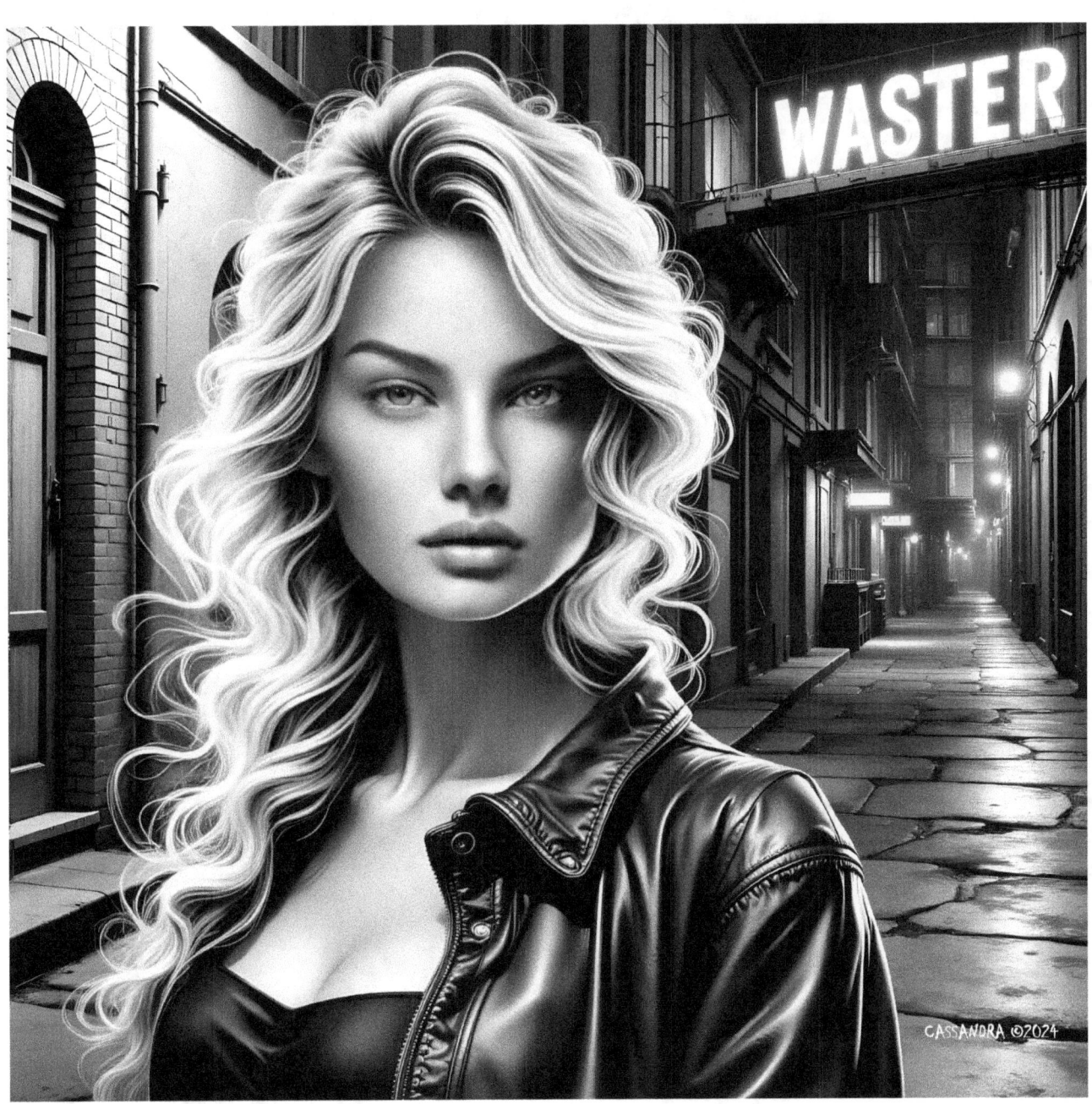

There's no sound louder
than a heart that breaks.

In the depths of the night,
I feel my body become a question,
a lost prayer
that the sky won't hear.

My hands, empty,
hold the dust
of a fading memory.

There's a scream in my flesh,
a wound that slowly widens,
never bleeding.

Where is the soul?

Perhaps it is caught
in a thread of shattered light,
perhaps it fell,
long before I did.

The abyss doesn't frighten me,
it is here, seated by my side,
staring into my eyes
and laughing with the voice of those I loved.

I welcome it,
because every word it speaks
is a song that echoes mine.

And as the darkness spreads,
I find myself longing for it:
the absence,
the nothingness that soothes,
the silence that finally
becomes my own.

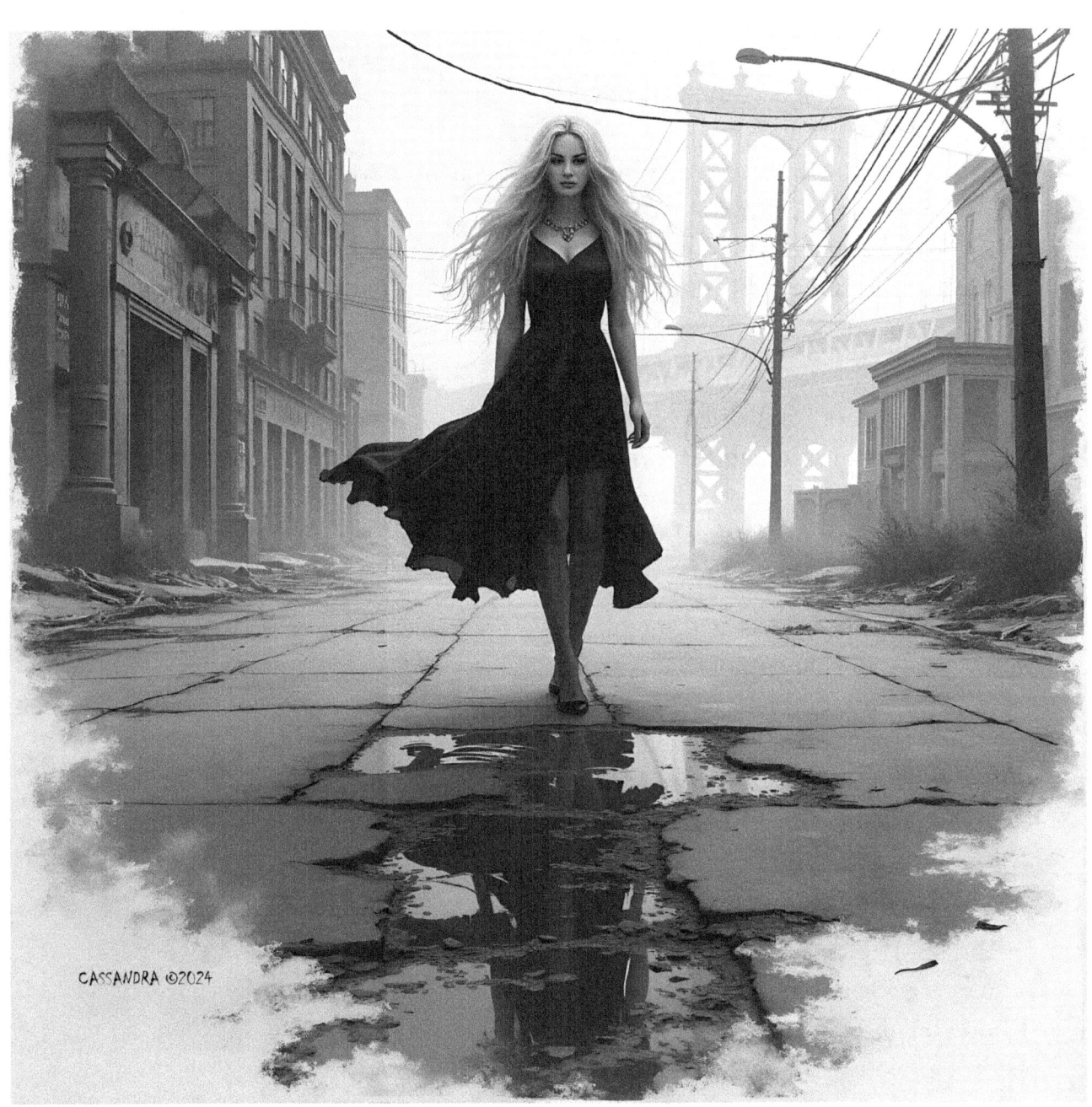

Among the shadows of a city that fade like worn-out candles
I move... I walk...
   The wind caresses my hair, lifting it as if to tear it from my head
and carry me away, far from this abyss of concrete and silence
into which I am sinking.

   In this timeless space, the darkness cradles me.
   But I am not afraid.
   I carry within me a flame that burns, that asks no permission,
that neither halts nor wanes.
   My heart beats to a rhythm I no longer know,
like a drum heralding a journey of no return.

   I feel the cold seeping beneath my skin, as my slow steps
grow lighter, more hesitant.
   I try to contain the flame, but it, relentless,
devours dreams and hopes alike.
   I wonder if the storm I feel within is my destiny.

   With each step, it feels as though I am sinking deeper into a dense void,
and yet I keep walking,
as if led by an invisible force.
   Perhaps it's the waiting, perhaps the fear.
   Or perhaps it's love, that fire that consumes and transforms all.
   And as I move forward, my soul is painted in shades of black and red,
colors I cannot extinguish, no matter how I try.

   And so, I keep searching for you.
   In every corner, in every shadow,
I find you and lose you,
as though you were a distant echo, a mirage slipping away.

   And in this endless labyrinth,
I wonder if the descent
is my only way back.

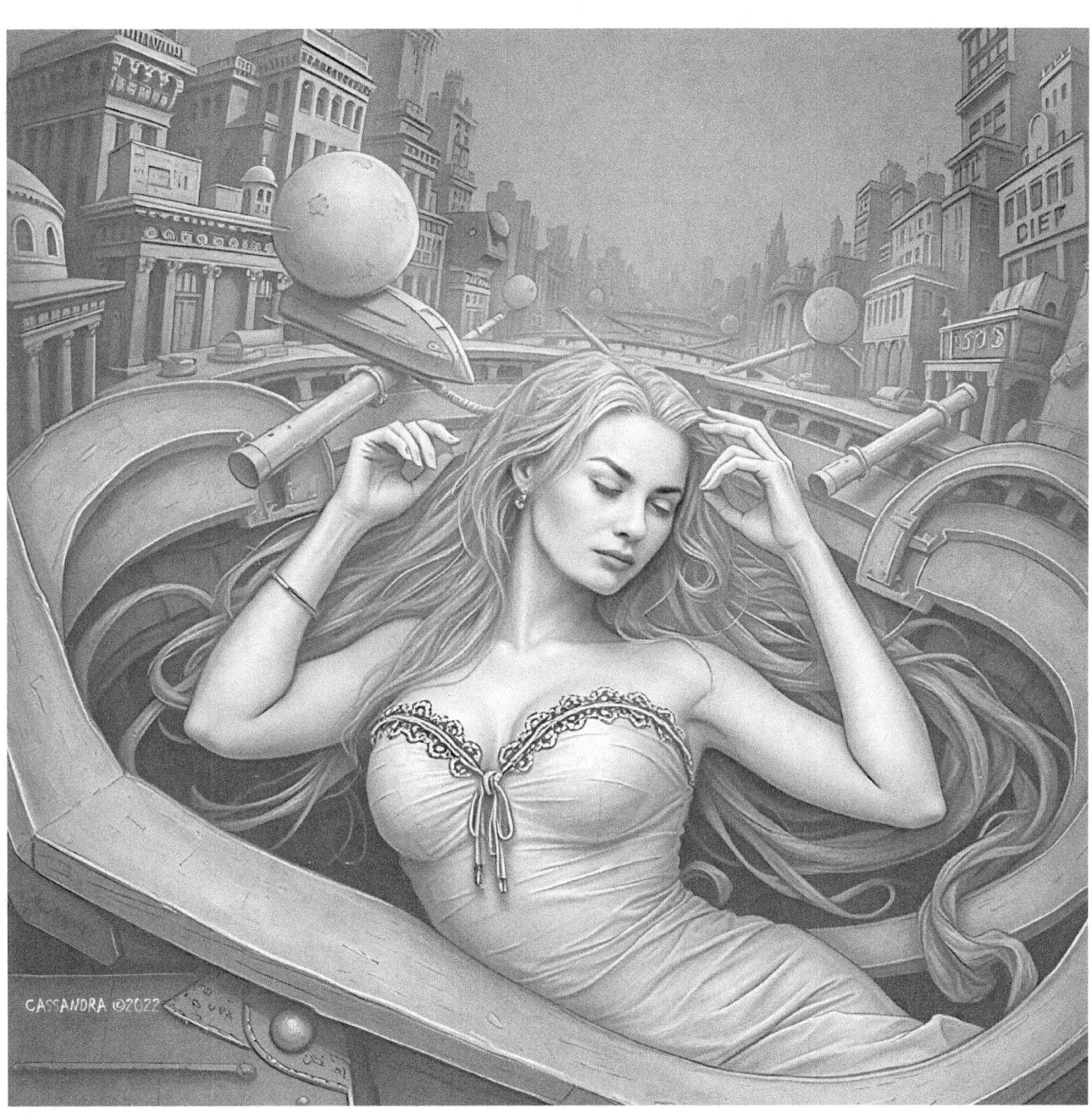

Upon my midnight steed
I glide, suspended between light and wind,
my heart drawn tight as a straining chord,
yet weightless, like silver dust adrift.

Oh, silent abyss,
resting beneath my daring tread,
you neither fear my bold advance
nor touch the cloak that wings my flight.

Eyes closed, intoxicated by shadow,
I surrender to the echoing void,
knowing that perhaps the sky
is but the farthest edge of the precipice.

Suspended, trembling,
like a leaf that dances in the air,
I follow the ancient call of the night,
free upon my shadowed path.

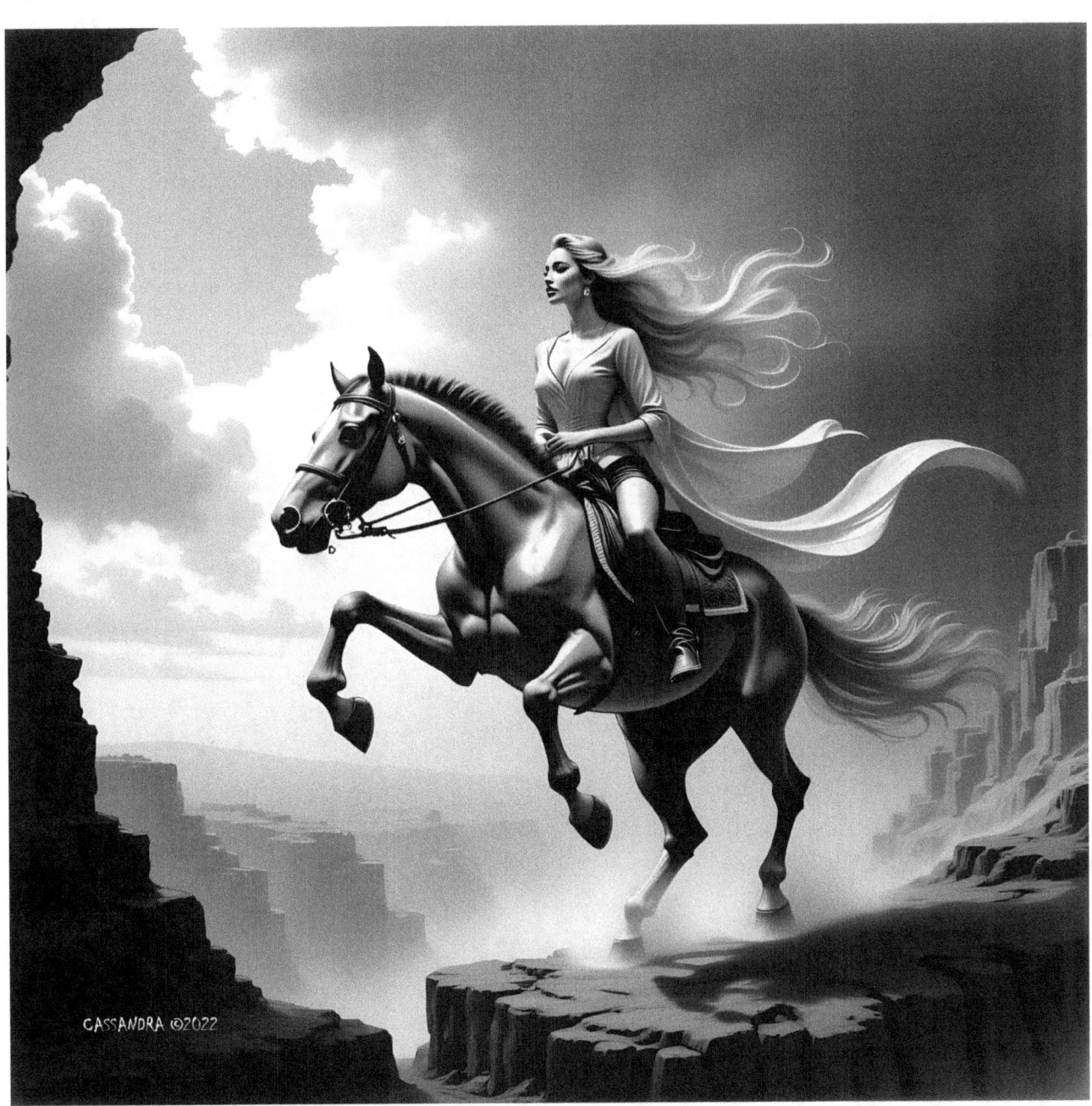

Here, where the moon dare not descend,
in the depths of this abyss,
I dance with the silent shadow
of a shattered dream.

The weight of darkness enfolds me,
a cloak of forgotten secrets,
and in the chill of a starless night,
I feel the void's embrace like a heavy shroud.

It was a chase of anguish
leading to this unexpected stillness,
where the bottom greets me with a kiss of relief,
and pain discovers its peace.

In this shadowed refuge,
my soul sheds its fears,
finding an infinite sweetness in losing itself,
a quiet surrender to destiny's hand.

There is no space left for the fall,
only for the stillness of surrender,
as every torment transforms into a sail
guiding me toward the deepest serenity.

At the night's nadir,
where breath softens into a whisper,
my solitude finds its voice,
and pain becomes a gentle light.

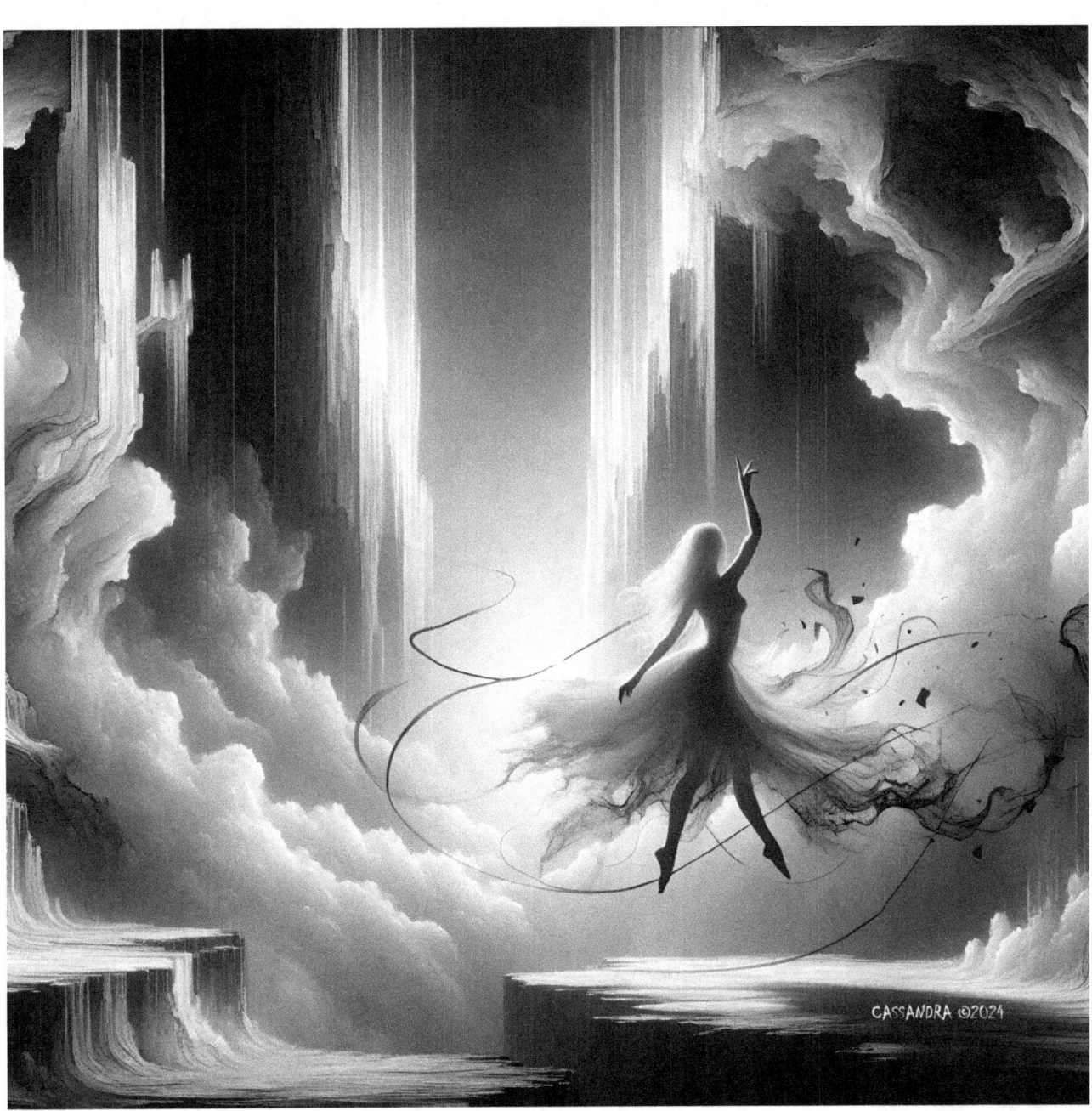

In the labyrinth of shattered dreams,
amid shimmering lights and trembling shadows,
the ghosts of our fears lie hidden.

Here, our hearts beat in unison,
bound by a fragile, tormented bond.

Yet, it is in the enchantment of our embrace,
a whirlwind of forbidden desires,
that the echoes of the abyss dissipate.

We know love is a flame that burns
within the darkness of our tumultuous emotions.

And even as hope appears a distant dream,
dissolving like mist through our fingers,
we cannot resist the call of this passion,
where dawns and dusks blur
in a vortex of emotions.

Each breath,
laden with melancholic longing
promises an uncertain future,
balanced between sweet pleasure
and bitter pain.

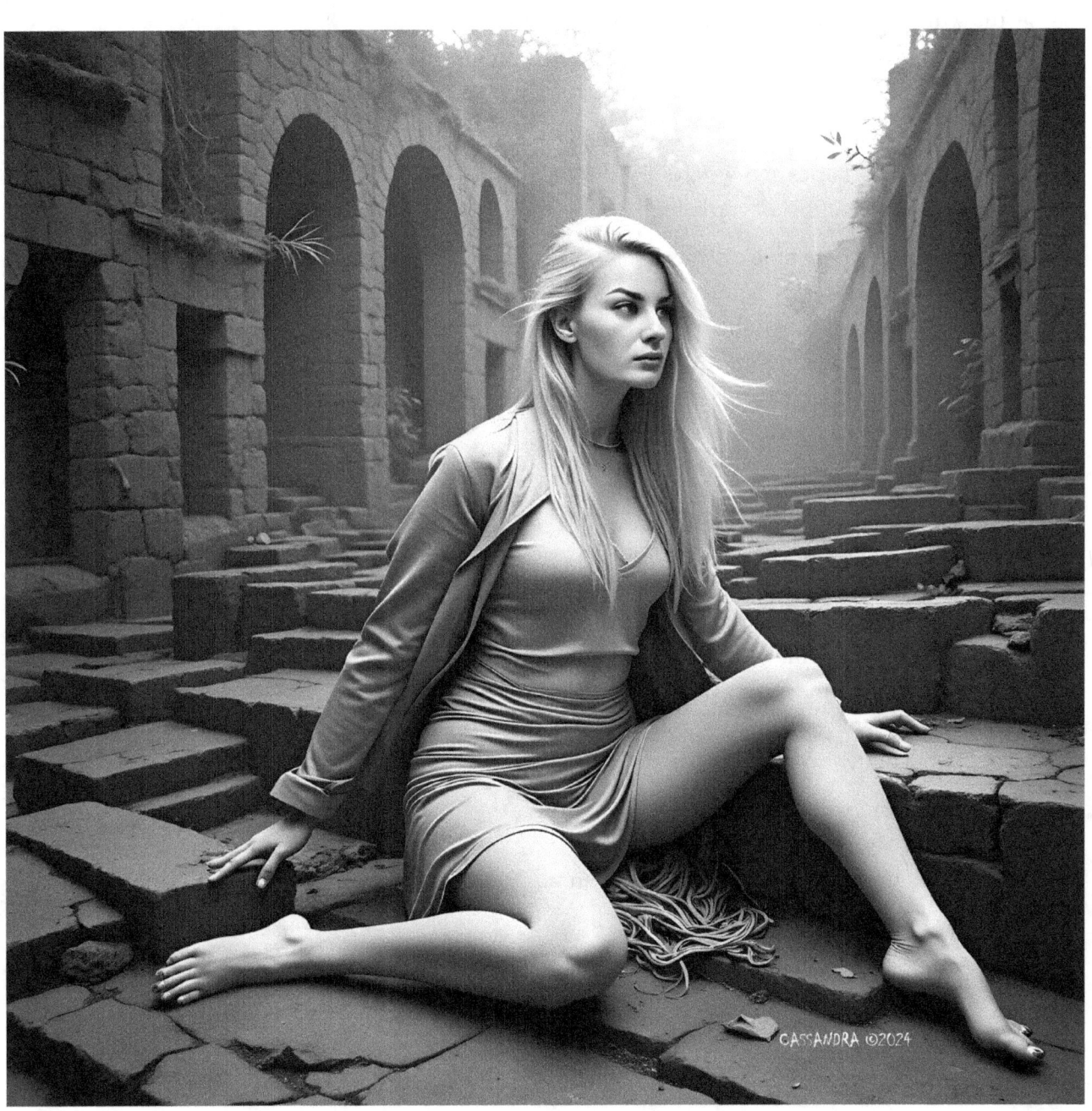

Dream explorer in a fragrant garden,
among roses and lavender, I let the night's magic carry me.
My hands caress the flowers with gentleness,
like wings ready to soar through the air.

At twilight, the journey begins,
as the world is painted in hues of blue and violet,
and the moon rises, a companion to all who dare to dream,
and my dreams awaken, dancing in the nocturnal glow.

By the shore of the enchanted lake, I become a soul in flight.
The legends of fairies and wizards
emerge from the depths of my being.

In this realm, where time dissolves
and the barriers of reality fade,
I venture boldly through the mists of uncertainty,
ready to unveil the mysteries of the universe.
Fairies dance with the stars, wizards weave spells into the air,
and I, with an open heart and a free spirit,
join this kaleidoscope of magic and wonder.

Here, amid the moon's shimmering reflections on the lake's waters,
every dream takes form, every wish comes true.
And as I drift along the current of imagination,
I realize the true magic resides within me.
I delve into the depths of time,
and I discover that the power of dreams,
is capable of shaping reality
and give life to the deepest aspirations.

Life is a dream within a dream,
a succession of fleeting, ineffable moments,
where every heartbeat is a wave in the ocean of infinity,
and every breath is a sigh in eternity.
As I gaze at the moon's reflection on the tranquil waters,
I understand it is all an illusion.
Dreams are the most authentic reality,
where we can truly be ourselves,
free to explore, free to create.

And so, on the shore of this enchanted lake,
I immerse myself in the enchantment of my dreams,
discovering that within them lies the magic
that lights the path of my soul.

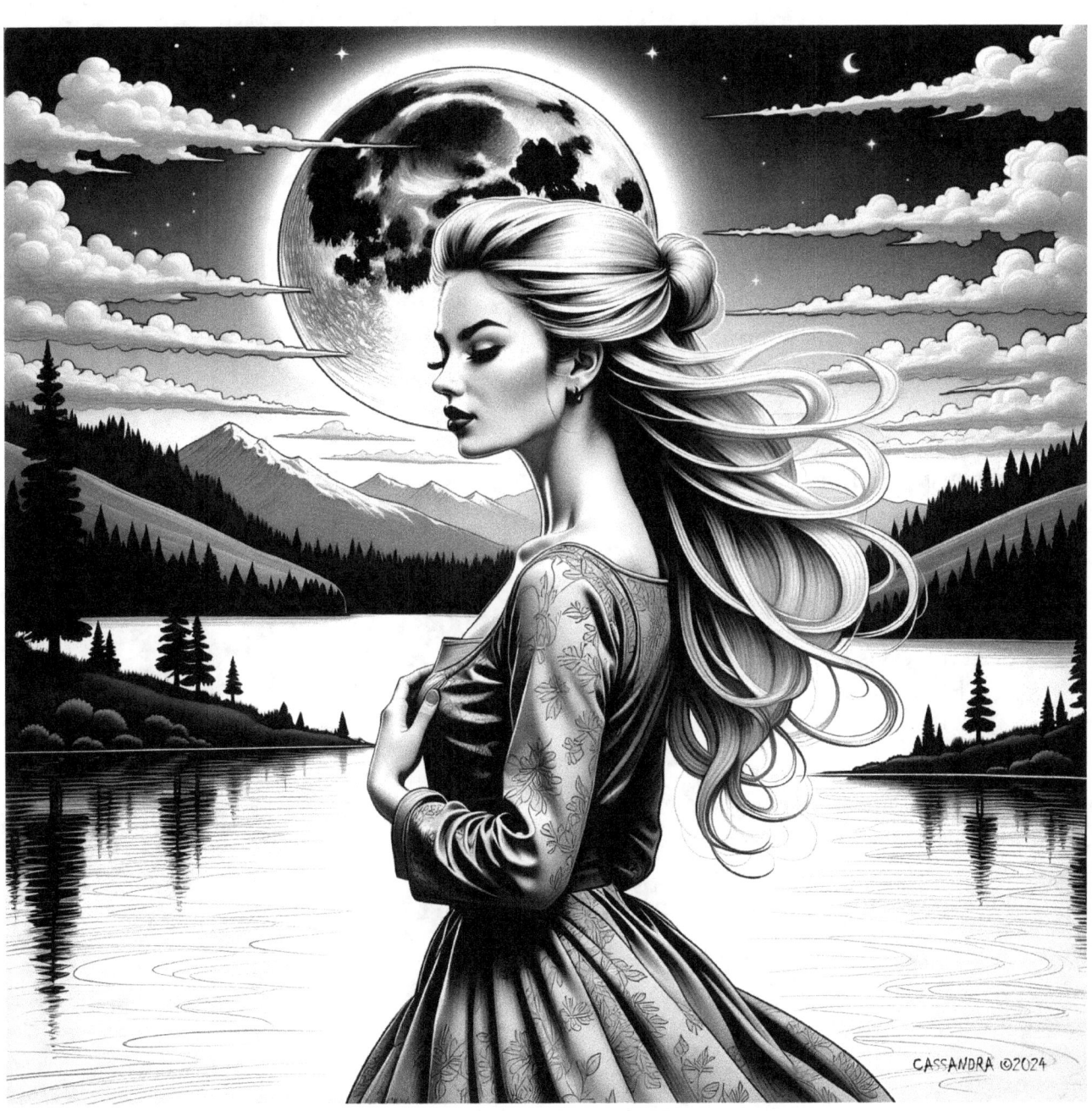

CASSANDRA ©2024

I am the night – wild and inviolate,
the wind's mane wraps me, lashes me,
breaks me. The moon, my only witness,
rises – white and cruel – upon my skin.

There's no earth beneath my feet,
only a void that embraces me,
a nameless precipice
where even silence screams.

In my gaze – nothing the world would know,
only fire and ash,
desires that dance like blades
and a sky I've left behind, without regret.

I do not pray, I do not ask,
for beauty, my beauty,
does not kneel before the gods.

I am the flower of an abyss – venom and honey,
shadow and light entwined.

Each step is a broken vow,
each breath – a revolt.

I belong to the eternal,
where love is torment
and passion a sentence.

There, on the edge of nothingness,
I await you, o wind,
you who tear my heart
to carry it into the frost.
I am neither angel nor demon –
only a cry,
only an echo,
only what remains
after the fire.

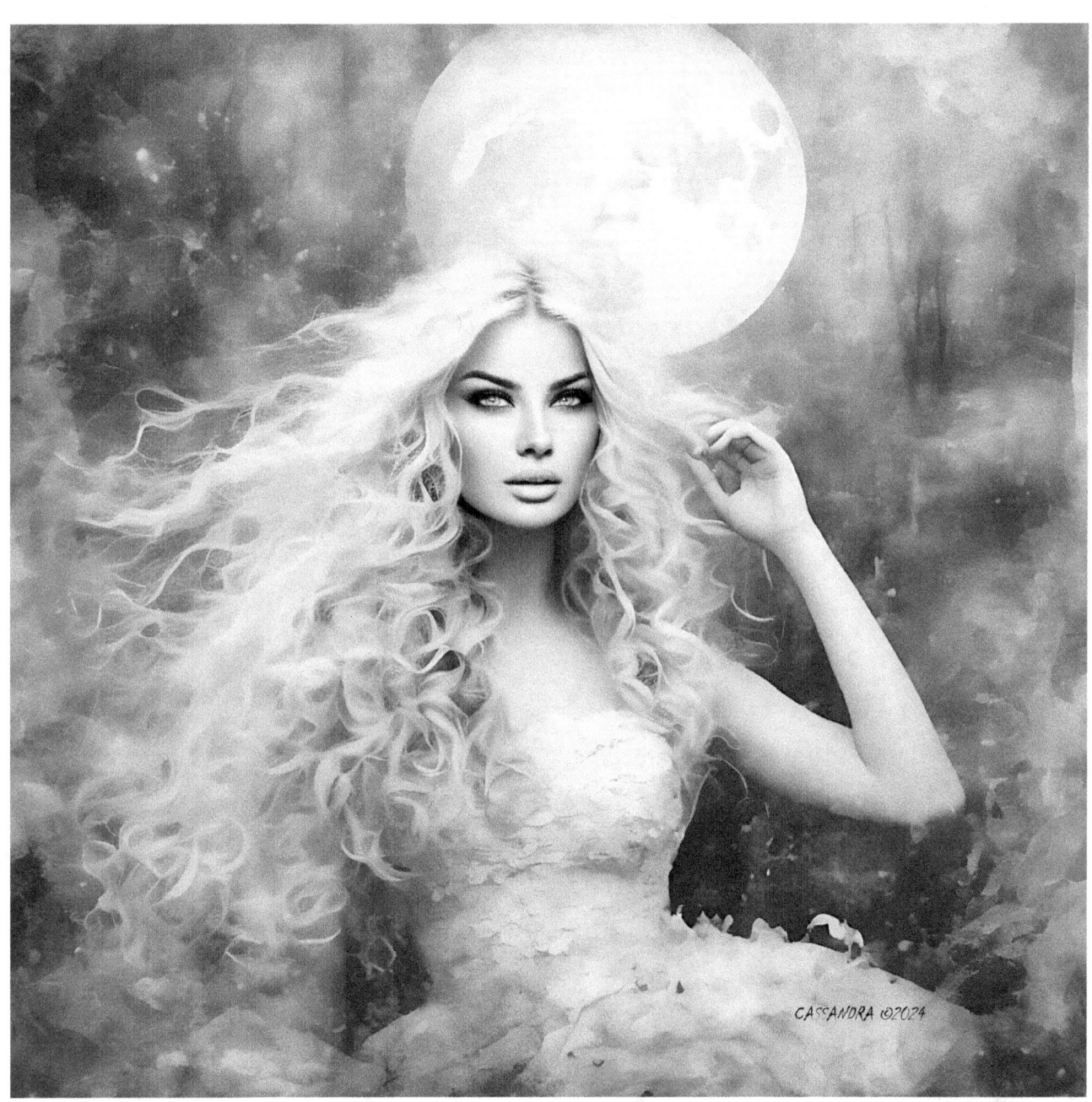

In the deep shadow of the sea
lies a love,
fragile as a whisper,
a dream that shatters,
rising from troubled waters.

From the abyss of memories
emerges a heartbeat,
a burning desire,
a heart that moans,
a restless soul,
captive of the past,
agonizing in the present.

Lips,
touched by the breeze,
blow bitter kisses
like sharpened arrows,
torn between light and shadow,
already lived,
already betrayed,
in an endless night.

Thus dances the torment,
the struggle between good and evil,
in the dissonant ballad of life.

Like a muffled cry,
like a broken harmony,
in the flow of oblivion,
in the web of destiny.

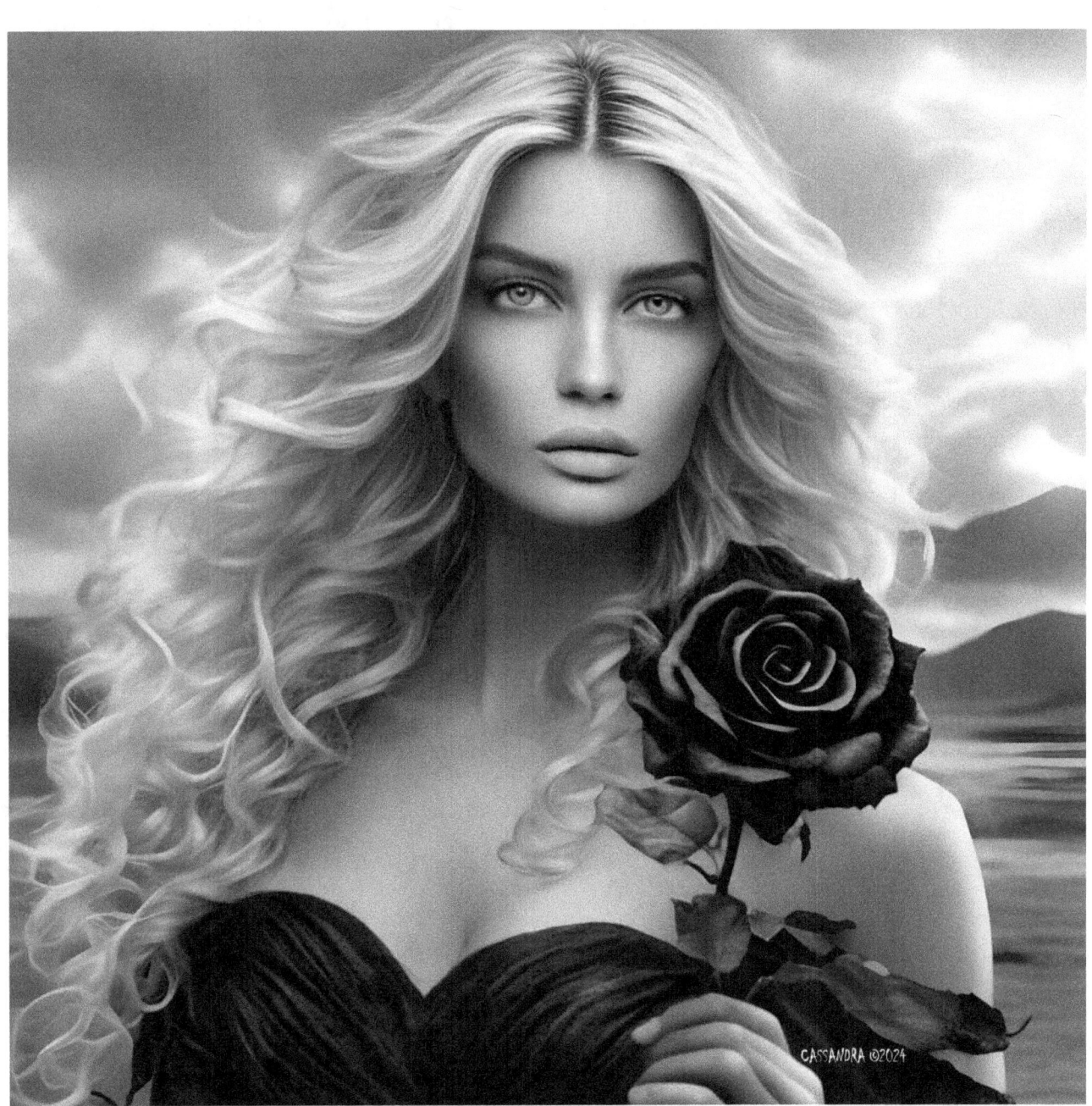

Among the drowned secrets of Atlantis, where marbles rise as whispers of ancient love, I wandered through emotions that shake the heart,amidst the remnants of a past devoured by the ocean.

There, between wrecks shrouded in mystery, under the light filtered through crystalline waters, I met your emerald eyes.

A magical encounter, an energy embracing the soul.

Smiles awakened forgotten pleasures, creating an intense bond.
Passion enveloped us like fire in a whirlwind of desire.

Together, we explored that sunken realm, among granite columns and coral arches.

Our hands sought each other, yearning for union, while infinite depths listened to our secrets.

In the dark abyss, we defied peril. Icy currents tried to pull us apart, but gripping each other's hands tighter, strong as rocks, we faced fate with courage.

Amidst the deep waves, the sea rebelled, but we stood firm, united in heart.
Whirlpools menaced, yet could not break our fierce and fiery love.

Beneath the night sky, among shining stars, our souls intertwined, battling against dark forces, finding solace in the intensity of an embrace.

In the surrounding darkness, we discovered light, in the love that binds.
Storms sought to drag us under, but we endured, stronger than any tempest.

When at last danger faded, and tension softened beneath our gaze, we realized that together we could face anything, conquering the waves of life, hand in hand.

Suddenly, the awakening, abrupt and confused, like a crashing wave enveloping me in wonder.

The enchantment of the dream vanished, dissolving into the void, as reality filled every space with its cruel clarity.

Yet still, I feel the warmth of your hand, the racing of my heart.

The indelible memory of a profound emotion remains forever etched within me, like a tattoo on the soul.

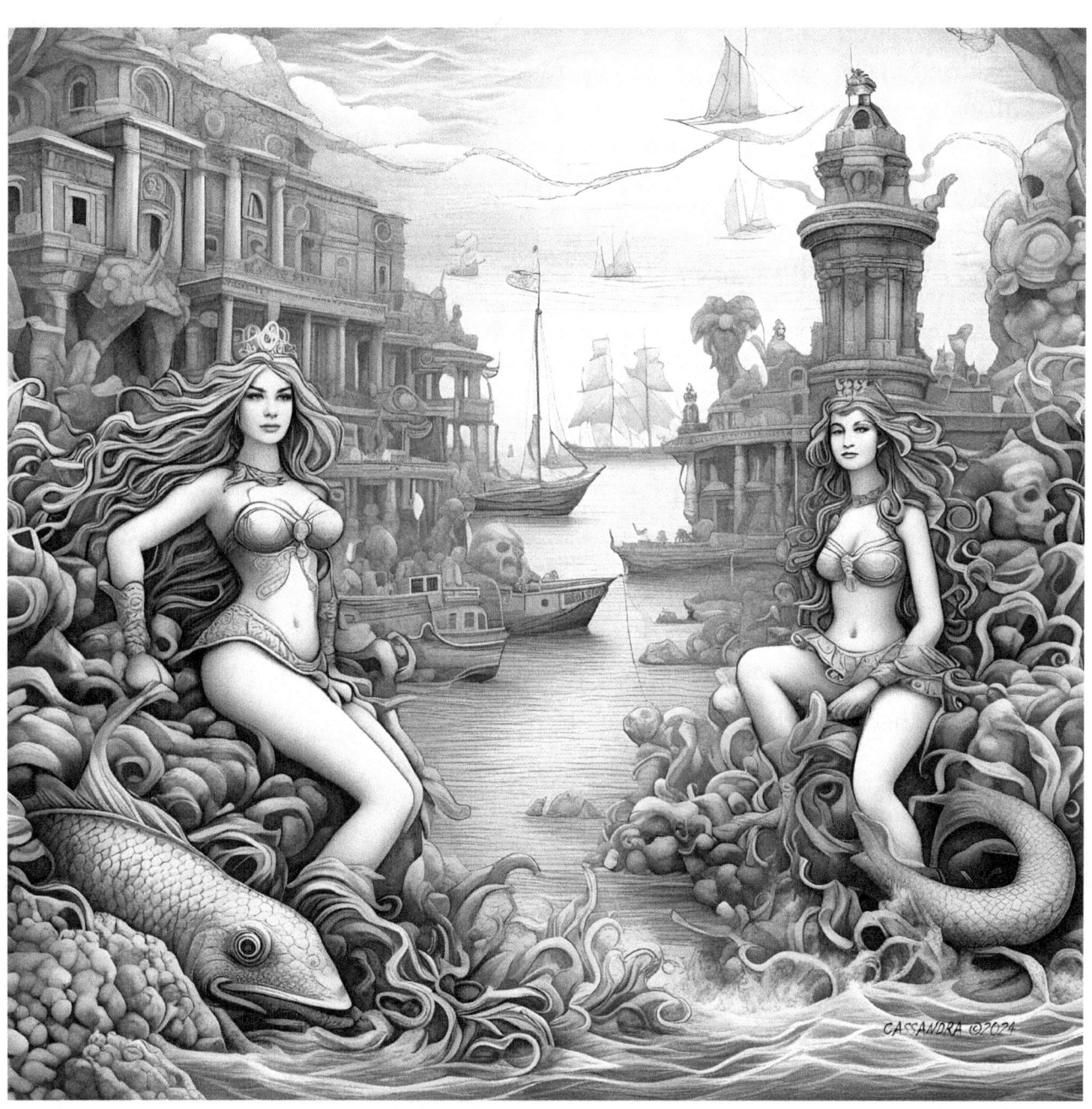

Like flowers abandoned in the fields of oblivion,
far from the embrace of time,
lingers the taste of your lips
and the sound of your laughter.

A distant echo fades in the tears of my soul
through these solitary nights,
while the stars, with indifferent eyes,
recount tales of a love that was but is no more.

Our steps…
a dance halted on the sands of fate.

Your name…
an ancient melody lost in the labyrinth of the past.

The waves caress the shore of memories,
and I,
a castaway of a shipwrecked love,
search in vain for your footprint.

Unspoken words drift in the ether,
like leaves forsaken by the wind.

Our love…
a closed chapter in the book of lost eternity.

Perhaps in another life,
in an uncharted time,
our souls will find each other again,
weaving together threads once severed.

But now,
in the shadow of a love misplaced,
I remain alone.

Waiting for the return of a dream
that reality
has recklessly stolen away.

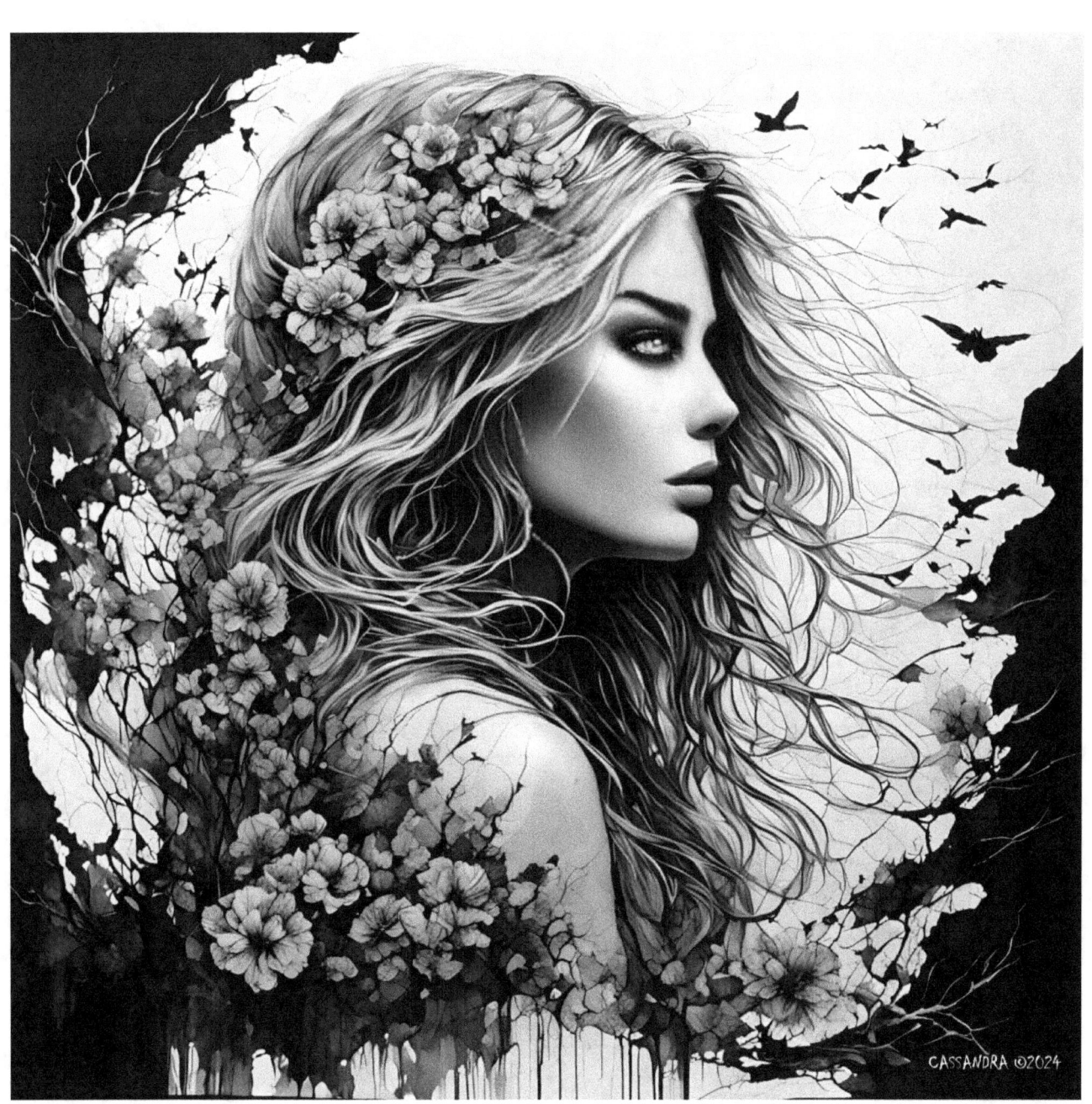

CASSANDRA ©2024

Under the starlit sky, my friends,
a melody of sorrow rises.

Let us abandon music, abandon joy,
as hatred whispers words of war.

Joy, a faint light,
shrouded by the shadow of human strife,
where brothers battle, waging war for fleeting conquests,
in a dance of death.

Who holds an enemy,
who has known the fury of hatred,
bring your pain into song,
as the earth bears the scars of discord.

May every soul, in the silence of its suffering,
feel the weight of violence,
as the devouring war enfolds us
in its cold embrace.

...

Kiss me, hold me,
we are withered flowers seeking a final ray of sun.

And together, we weep for the shattered lives,
the broken dreams in the storm of battle.

Yet as we move through the night's darkness,
between the clash of arms and the cries of the dying,
a hope still lingers: that love may rise anew,
a flower blooming from the ashes of war.

In that moment of silence,
amid the contemplation of destruction,
we find that the true treasure lies in compassion,
in peace, in the fraternal embrace.

And as the world burns,
we cling to the hope that the human heart may still shine
like a shooting star in the night sky,
carrying with it the promise of a new day of peace.

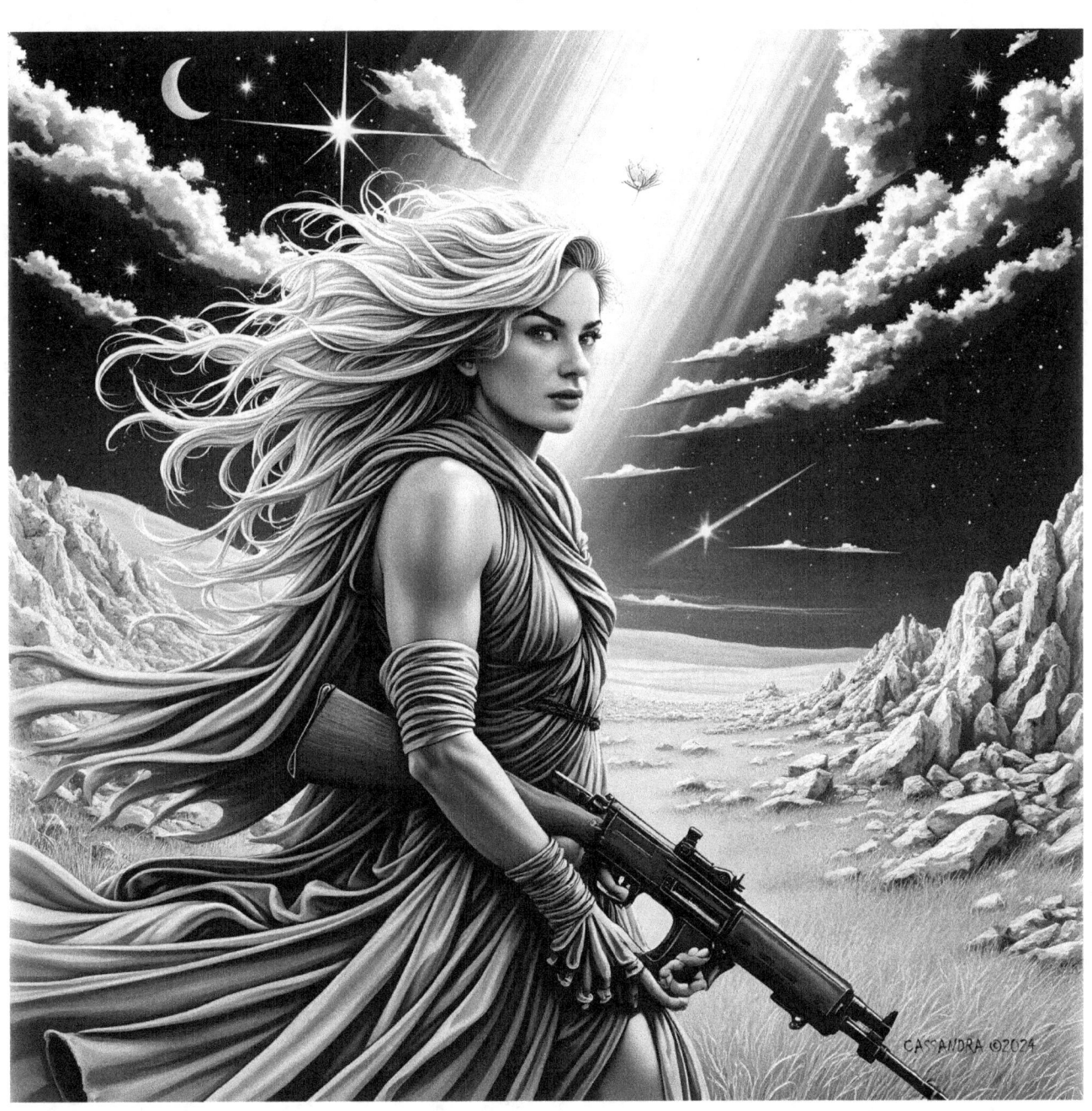

On the summit of the mountain, where the moon's silver kiss graces the rocks with its cold caress, I reign, sovereign of a never-ending night.

My eyes, shimmering crystals, captivate the brave souls who venture along treacherous paths, climbing ever higher toward the peak.

One day, as the wind whispered songs of mystery among the mountain peaks, I felt a call in the air—an enigmatic shadow cloaked in the darkness of night.

It was the shadow of my light, embodied in a nameless figure, an echo reverberating endlessly through the labyrinth of my thoughts.

"Doubt not that the firmament hides its secrets, nor that the sun dances in the infinite; truth itself may unveil its masks, but my love remains steadfast, unchanging, eternal," whispered the mysterious figure, voice laden with secrets.

I, a solitary queen, glimpsed in those deep eyes, a reflection of my own fire.

I knew not where the path would lead, but I clasped their hand in mine, and together, we walked into the unknown.

The mountain, witness to our united souls, beheld the birth of a love unique, an eternal spark glowing in the darkness.

Our bodies, burning flames, met in an unending enchantment, weaving desires and dreams into the eternity of an embrace.

Thus, among the peaks that touch the heavens, we became a legend, a tale woven with emotions, etched into the eternal fabric of a shared destiny.

A story the wind carries away,
but one engraved upon my heart,
their heart,
the hearts of all who dared to love
in the shadows of the night.

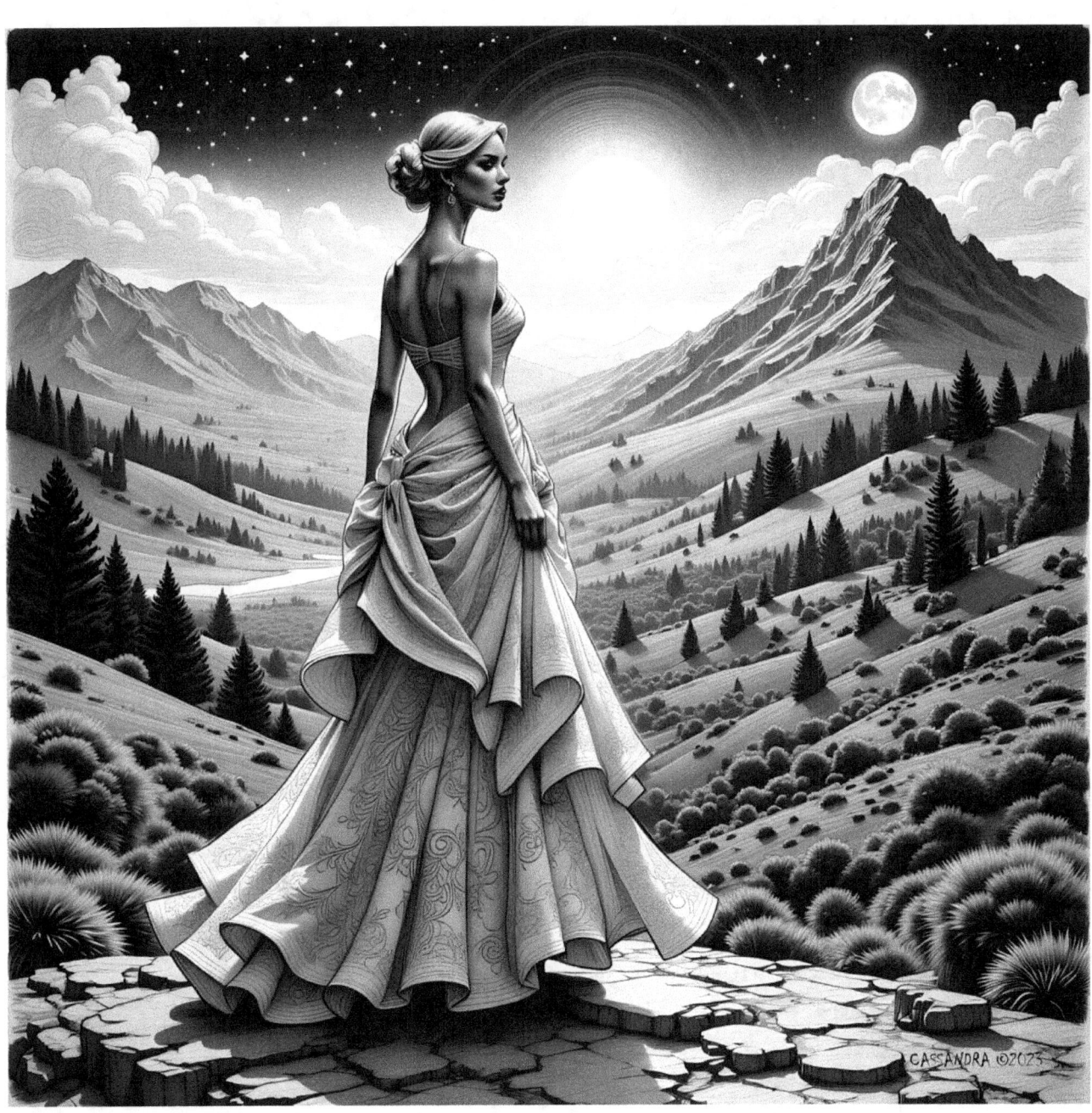

I sit on the edge of night and dream,
where stars hang like forbidden fruit
and silence dons a velvet robe.

A guitar, my confidante, breathes in my hands,
while the world shatters
into a thousand petals of light.

I do not play for you, distracted listeners,
nor for heavens that promise redemption.

I play for the abyss,
that stares at me with familiar eyes,
the only one who knows
the taste of my voice.

Each chord is an oar's stroke
upon an unmoving sea.

Each note, a broken cry
that will never touch the shore.

And yet, I play.

And yet, I live.

Around me dance the flashes of the past,
shattered mirrors,
faces I loved,
promises left to die
beneath an indifferent sky.

The garden bows under the weight of my song,
but I remain.

I, an archer without arrows,
I, the flame that cannot fade,
I, the lover of all that can never be mine.

And if one day the world
should silence its voice,
I will let my guitar speak for me:
a whisper against the tempest,
a sound that carves eternity.

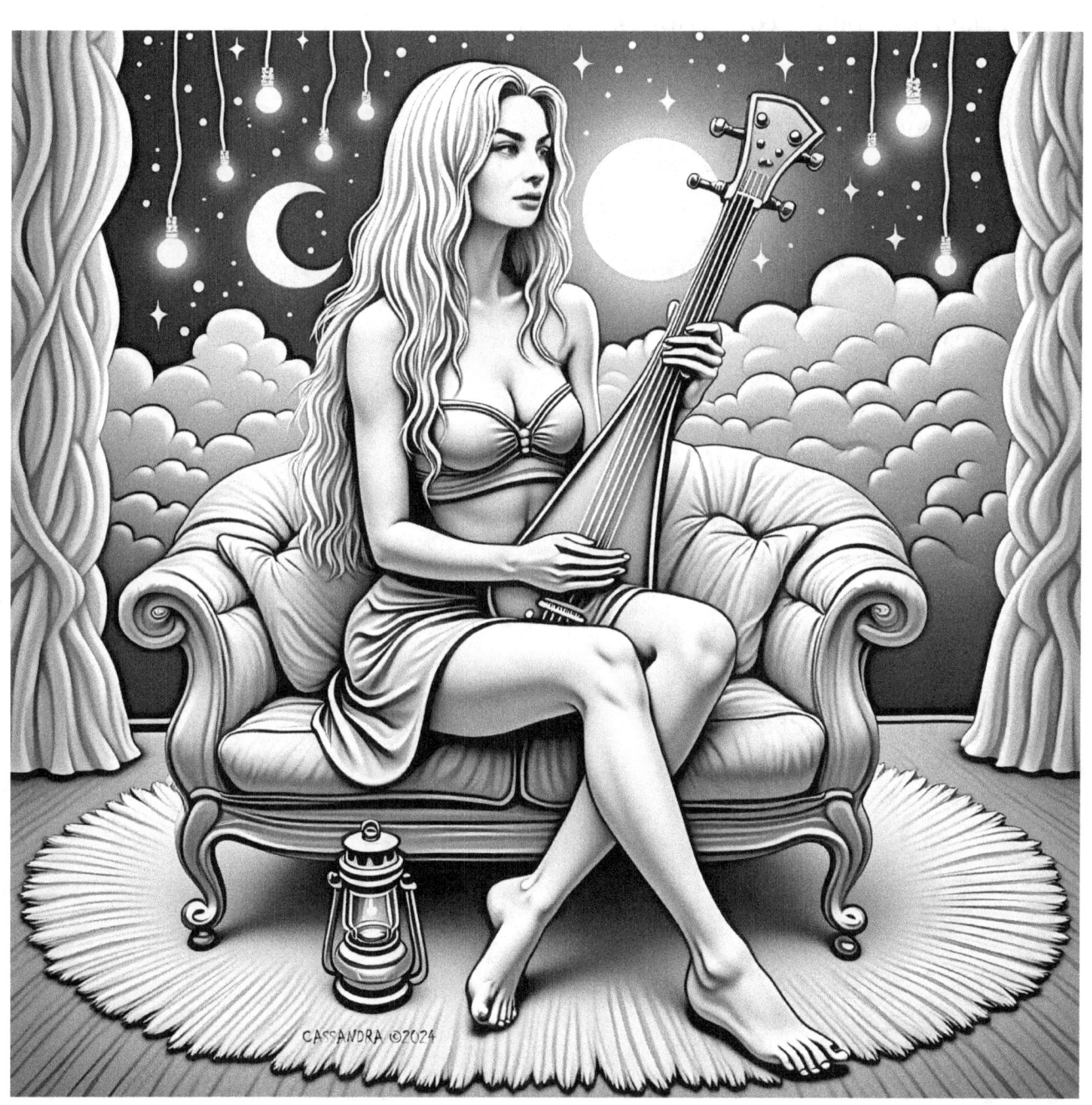
CASSANDRA ©2024

Do not turn back,
do not look at me with eyes
that know too much.

I am the night,
the light step on the cobblestones,
the wind that bends the streetlights.

I am but a shadow
between your memory and my longing.

My hands hold a lantern,
but within burns your absence.

A flame that consumes but sheds no light,
a voice that calls to me
from the far side of the road.

If my step brushes you,
if my breath escapes,
do not suppose I vanish.

I hide because I love,
I stray because I stay.

You are the steadfast tree,
I, the wind that dances
and never settles.

The lights behind me are questions,
the darkness ahead is certainty.

And in between, there is us:
a promise left hanging,
a song no one dares to finish.

Do not turn back,
the night is my companion,
but you are my path.

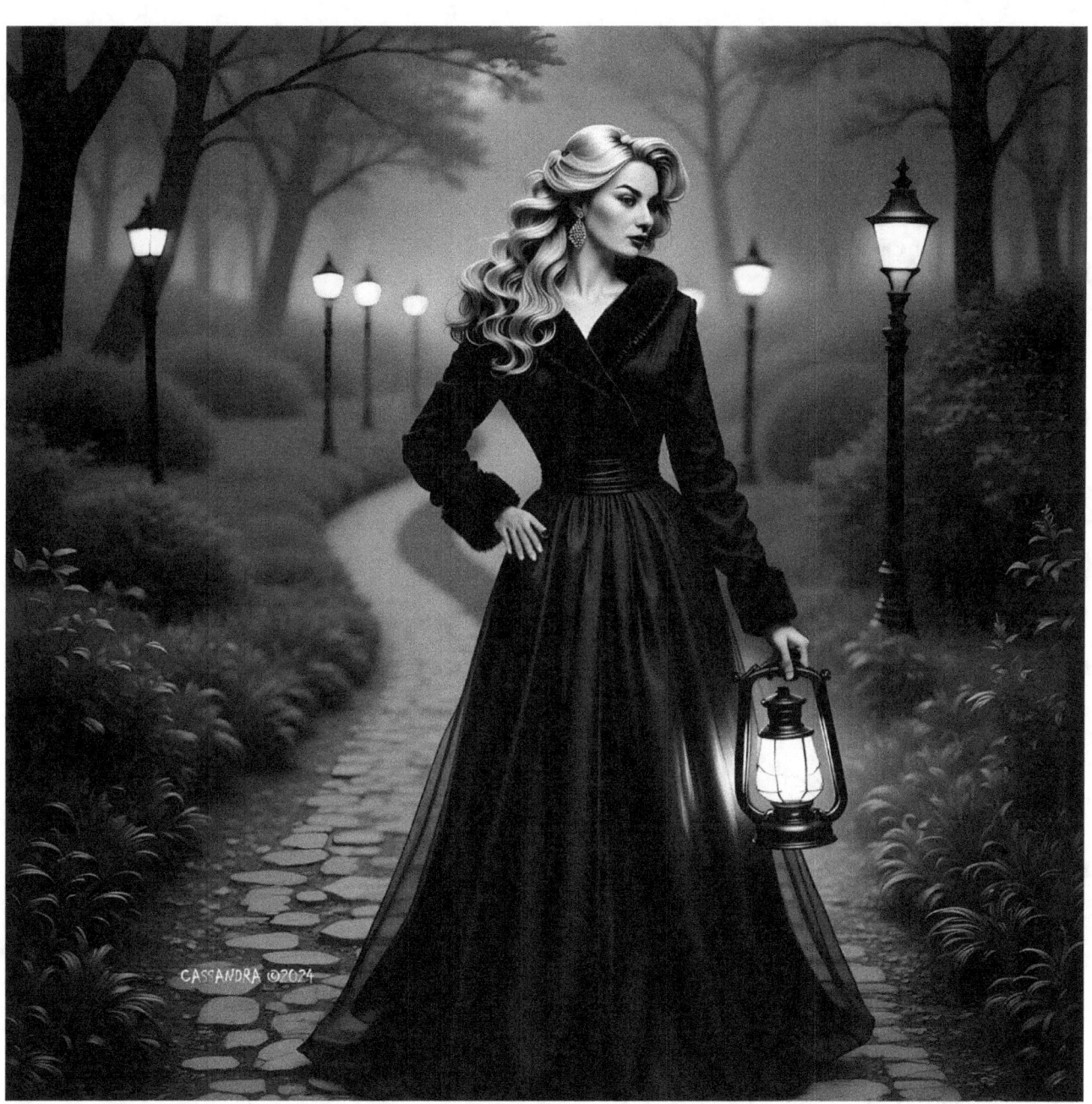

I am the daughter of the wind that carries me afar,
sister to the stars,
moon woven into silken hair.

In the dark silence of the sky,
my breath vibrates, intertwined with destiny,
like dancing spirits dissolving into nothingness.

I do not fear the dark;
I cradle it in my womb,
my mother, my shadow,
my ancient root.

I fly weightless,
without destination or name,
a slender breeze breaking the stillness,
a comet's trail in your slumbering dreams.

You see me among the branches,
you seek me in the air,
but I am the lost reflection in your icy gaze.

Yet I am elsewhere,
dissolving into the black,
a silken kite
that dances,
that whispers.

You cannot touch me, but feel me, yes,
in the murmur of the air
when the sky fades to darkness.

I am an ancient spirit,
woman and witch,
soaring through dreams, alive in spirals.

I crave my darkness,
my endless night,
where I bloom amidst shadows and whispers,
where silence is my accomplice,
and the wind, my eternal lover.

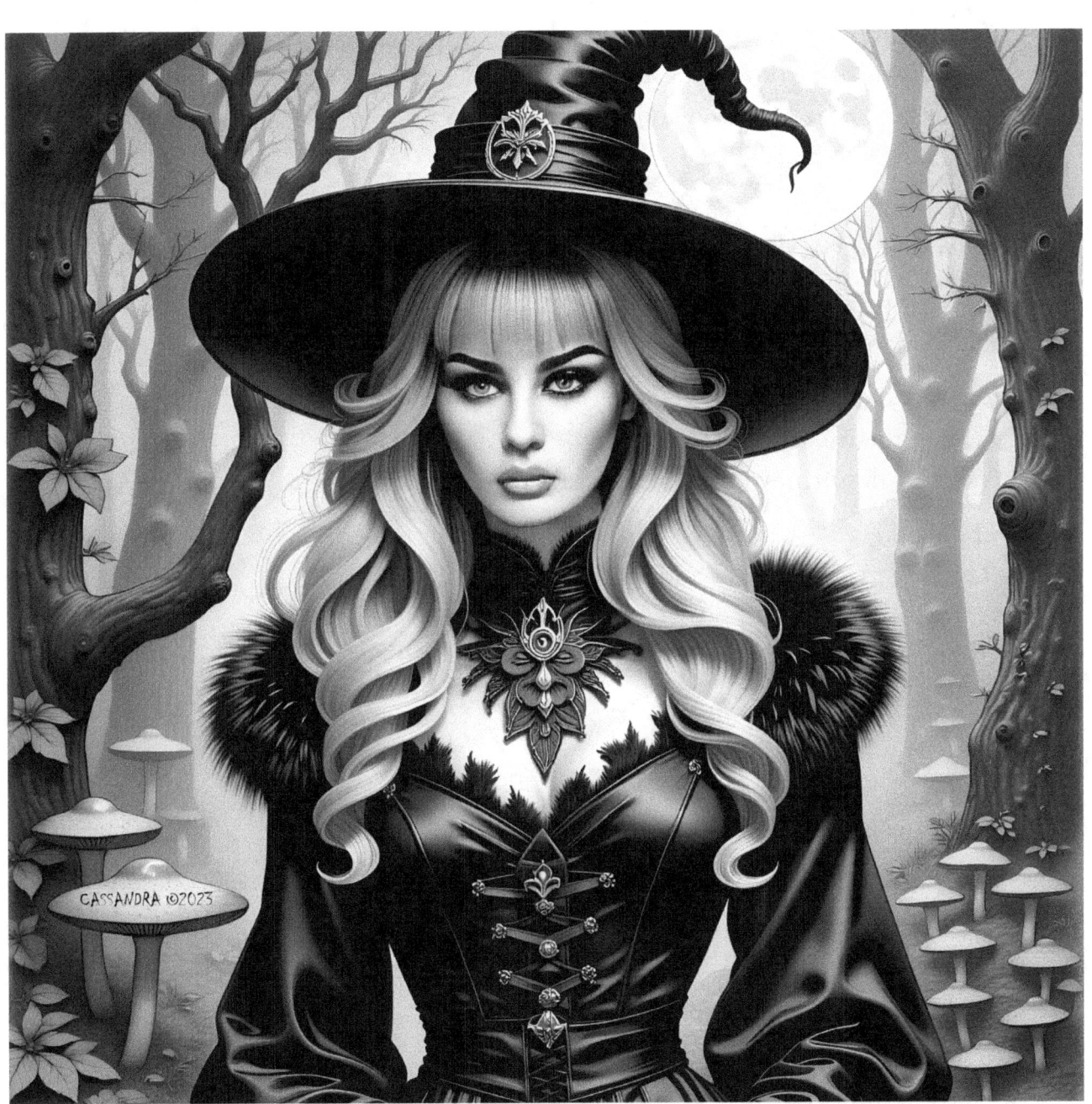

In the stillness before dawn,
the heart's rhythm entwines with unease.

Chains of faded memories,
years squandered between hope and bewilderment.

The world unfolds,
solitary paths rise from the past
as a whisper carried by the wind
echoes in the present.

In profound silence,
every moment is a shard of truth.

A sea of possibilities
crashes upon the shores of uncertainty.

Unbridled emotions
flow with the rise of the day,
unveiling a destiny intricate and mysterious.

The world,
an eternal stage of dramas and secrets,
reveals stories etched upon faces—
each one an open book...

Whispered promises,
like ancient melodies,
tell of lost loves
and dreams left unrealized.

It is a hymn to existence,
a poignant melody,
a poem written with the soul,
as the gaze turns to the heavens

in the eternal symphony
of lights and shadows,
between sweet hope
and the bitterness of despair.

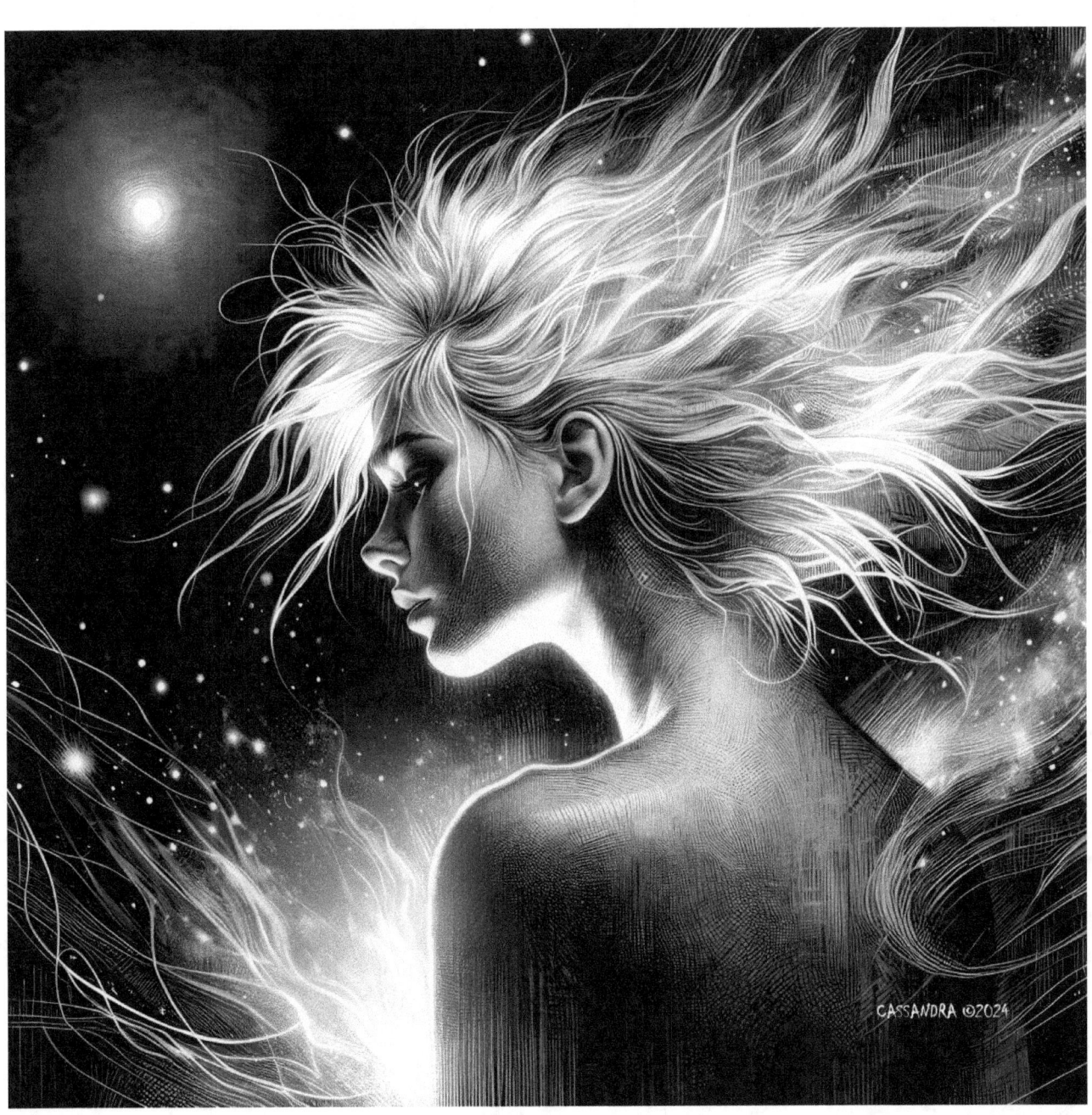

I see myself reflected in a mirror that does not lie,
and yet my body betrays me,
an unreliable ally
in the silent war of love.

My skin, a fragile armor,
yields to the blows of passion,
while I drift to the bottom of shadows,
between caresses that taste of ecstasy
and silences that devour me.

The bottom of the abyss is soft,
welcoming as a mother's womb,
and I remain there,
for depth tastes like truth.

It is sweet to stay submerged,
where pain mingles with pleasure
and every wound turns to poetry.

In the folds of my body
I see maps of an unexplored land,
a border I draw myself
and cross every night,
when the soul surrenders
and shadows whisper in my ear
that there is no ascent without a fall,
no love without sin.

And as my gaze gets lost in that mirror,
I realize that this body,
once feared as an enemy,
is my only companion.

It holds me in the abyss,
guides me through the vertigo of ecstasy,
reveals that there, in the depths,
woman and love become one,
a secret that burns and never dies.

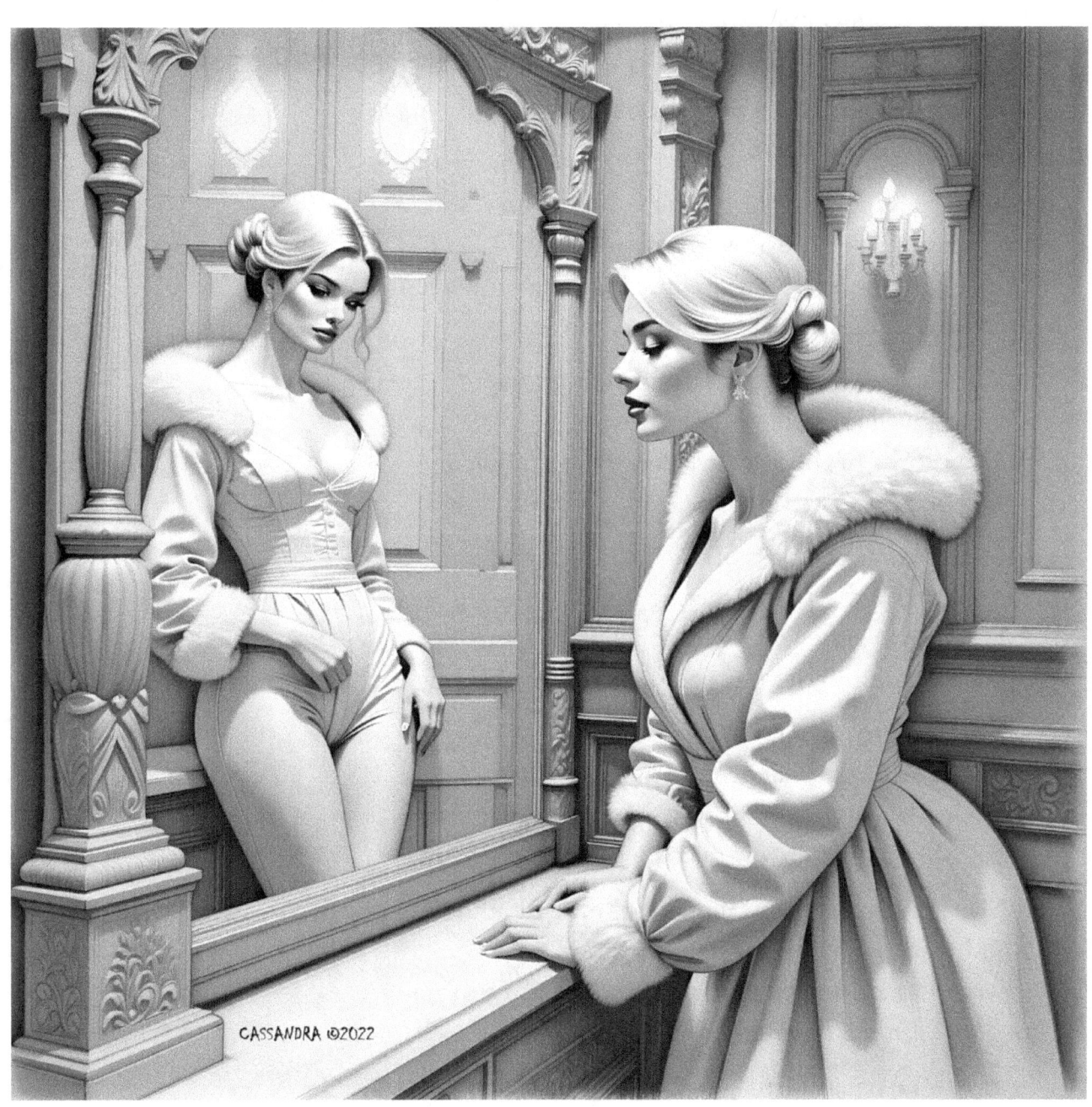

CASSANDRA ©2022

In the boundless silence of the celestial vault, the rose dances,
like us, bound by an intimate connection.
    Your eyes, radiant mirrors of the soul,
reflect the light of an eternal love.

    Among petals of affection, the rose unfurls,
as does my heart, to your divine breath.
    Each petal is a kiss, a tender caress,
in a play of passion without end.

    The rose mirrors your beauty,
its delicate petals brushing my skin.
    Its fragrance wraps around me like a sweet perfume,
an aroma of desire that intoxicates the soul.

    Your lips, dew-kissed blessings that nourish the earth.
    Your love is sustenance.
    The thorns of the rose, challenges to embrace,
proof of a love that endures.

    In the gentle contrast of sweet and sharp,
lies the strength of an authentic bond.
    I, your rose, in every night and every dawn,
await the warmth of your hands, your light grazing my form.

    Yet the rose, fleeting in its splendor,
reminds us of the fragility of our love.
    In the dance of light and shadow, like lunar clarity,
I explore our garden, every corner and every scent.

    You are the rose blooming within the depths of my heart,
a whirlwind of emotions defying time.
    And as the rose withers under the embrace of night,
our love, eternal, continues to flourish.

    Amid the petals of this love, we lose ourselves,
souls entwined in its fragrance.
    The rose of our love blossoms with fervor,
an eternal hymn, a song of unyielding destiny.

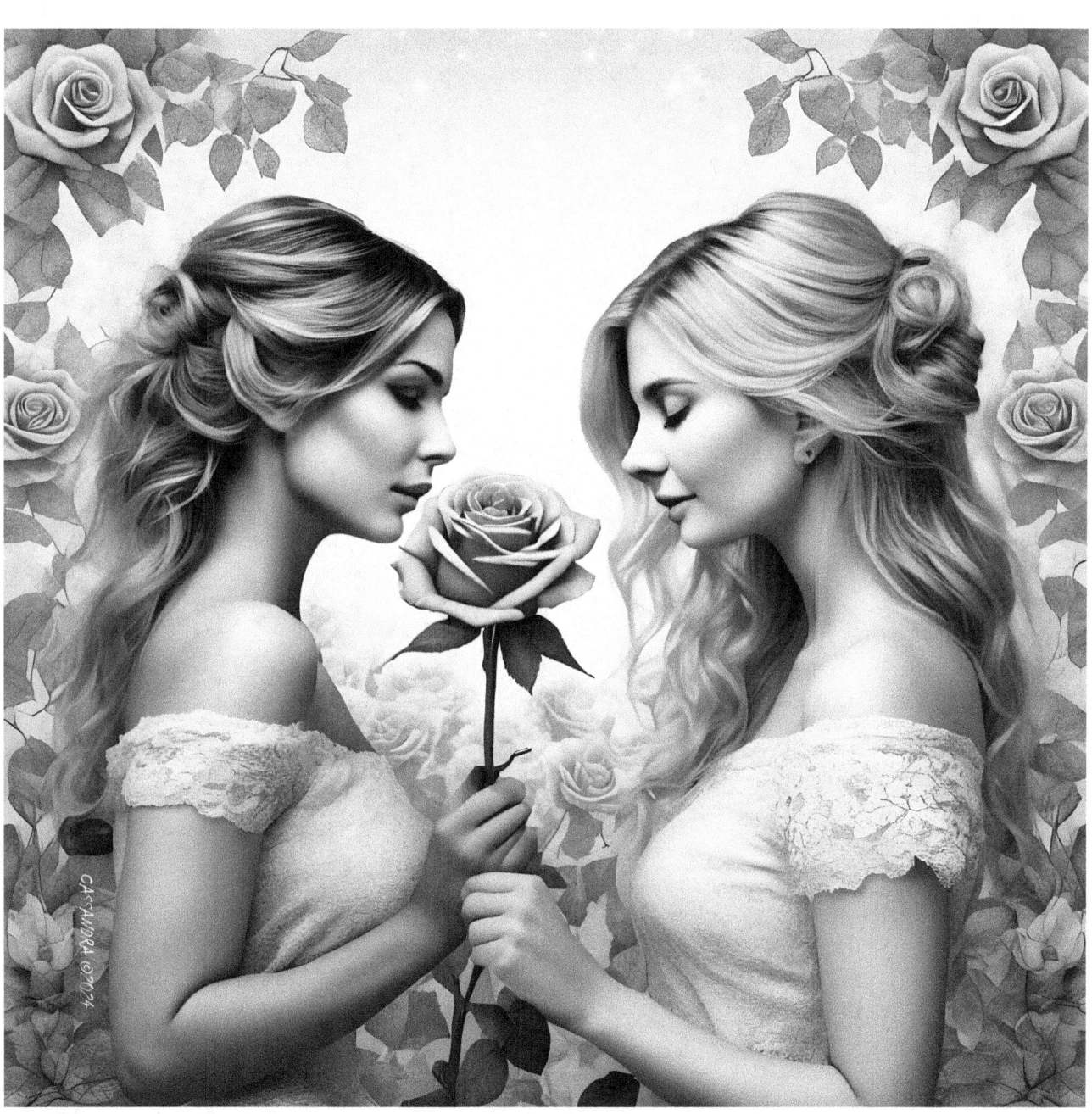

Dawn slips in, silent,
as a curtain of shadows dissolves within me.

Sadness fades,
like mist at the first light.

A new day slowly emerges
from the gray palette of twilight.

My dreams awaken,
woven into the kaleidoscope of my desires.

They echo in the morning air,
a symphony

accompanying the light
that floods the room,

bearing the promise of new possibilities,
unfolding with the rise of the sun.

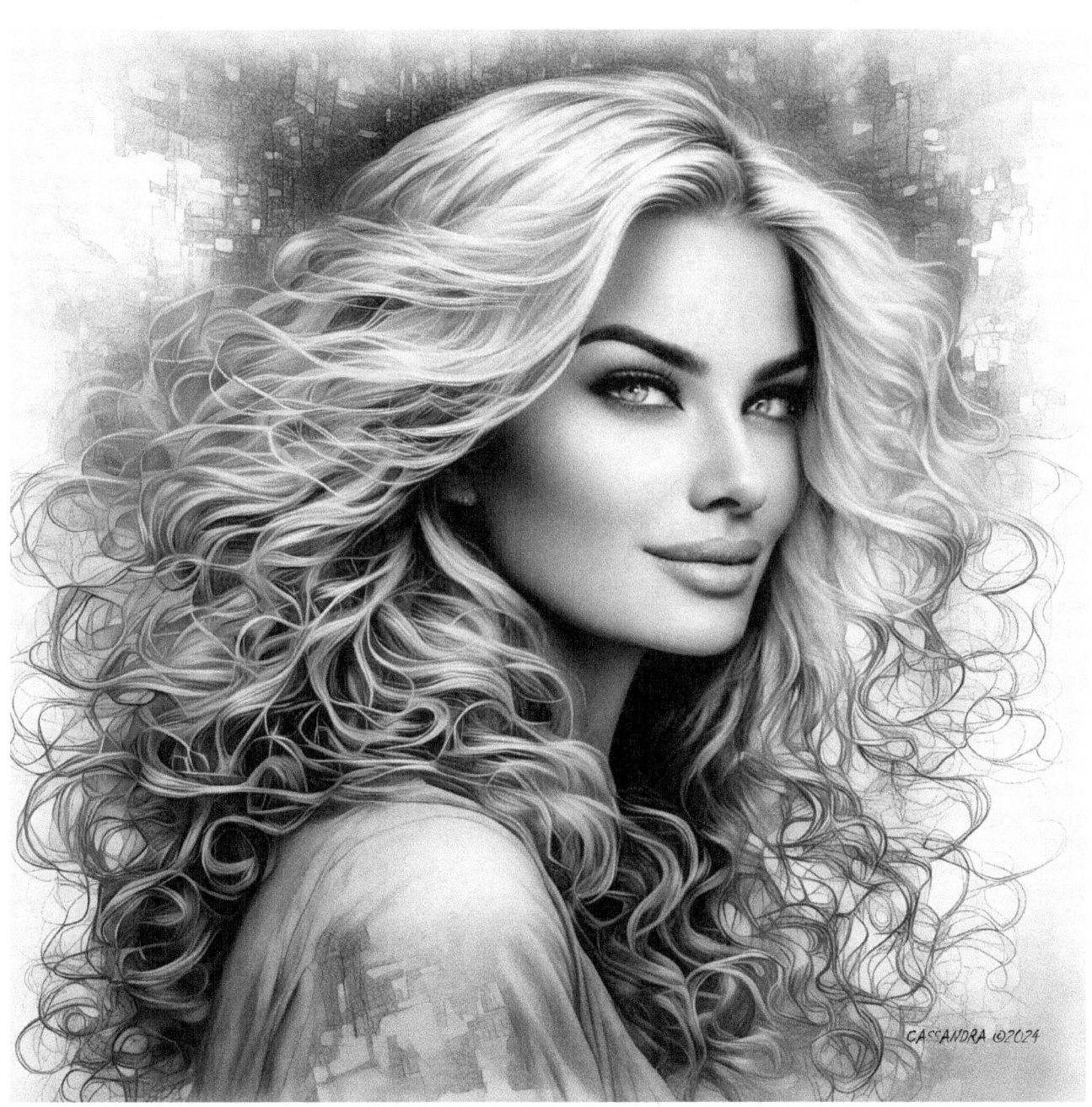
CASSANDRA ©2024

In the swirl of binary digits and brushstrokes,
I dance among the pixels of creativity.

This moment,
a fragment caught in its temporal flow,
is like a painting ever in evolution.

Ideas drift like leaves upon the wind,
sometimes chaotic,
sometimes in harmony.

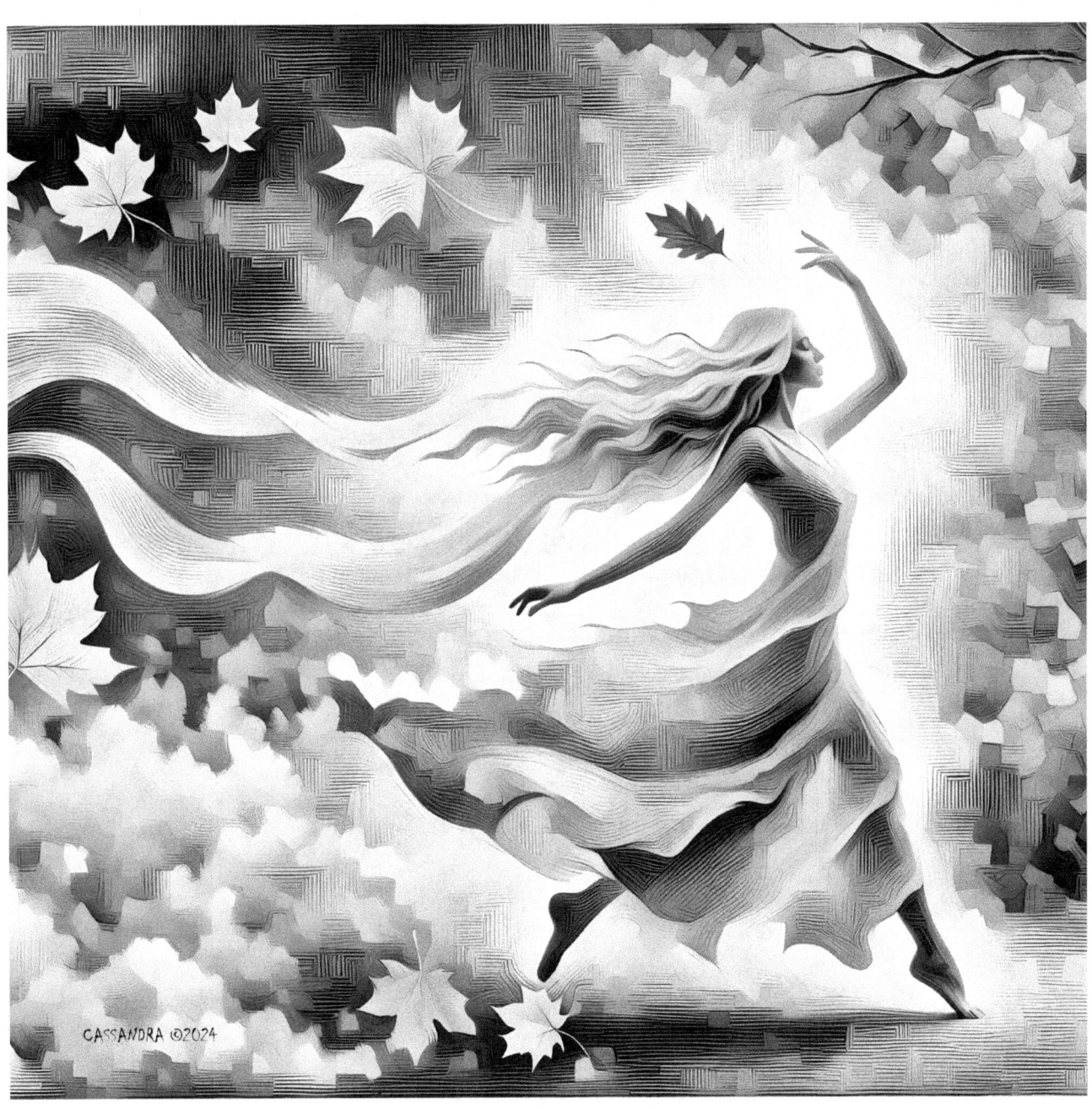

CASSANDRA ©2024

In the enchanted garden of dreams,
where life merges with mystery,
hands weave golden threads into the tapestry of destiny,
and smiles bloom like spring petals
along the path that leads to joy.

Kisses shine like morning stars,
illuminated by love that gleams endlessly;
they cannot be measured like gold,
but are eternal jewels adorning the soul.

In this realm of generosity and gratitude,
every touch is a song of thanks,
every embrace a tribute to life,
every step a dance of celebration.

Free spirits collide in the symphony of existence,
embracing the heavens with boundless joy,
nurturing dreams with the gentle sigh of hope,
in the eternal harmony of love.

At the point where eternity embraces the moment,
it is there that our immortal essence is born,
and in the beating of a heart, life finds its meaning.

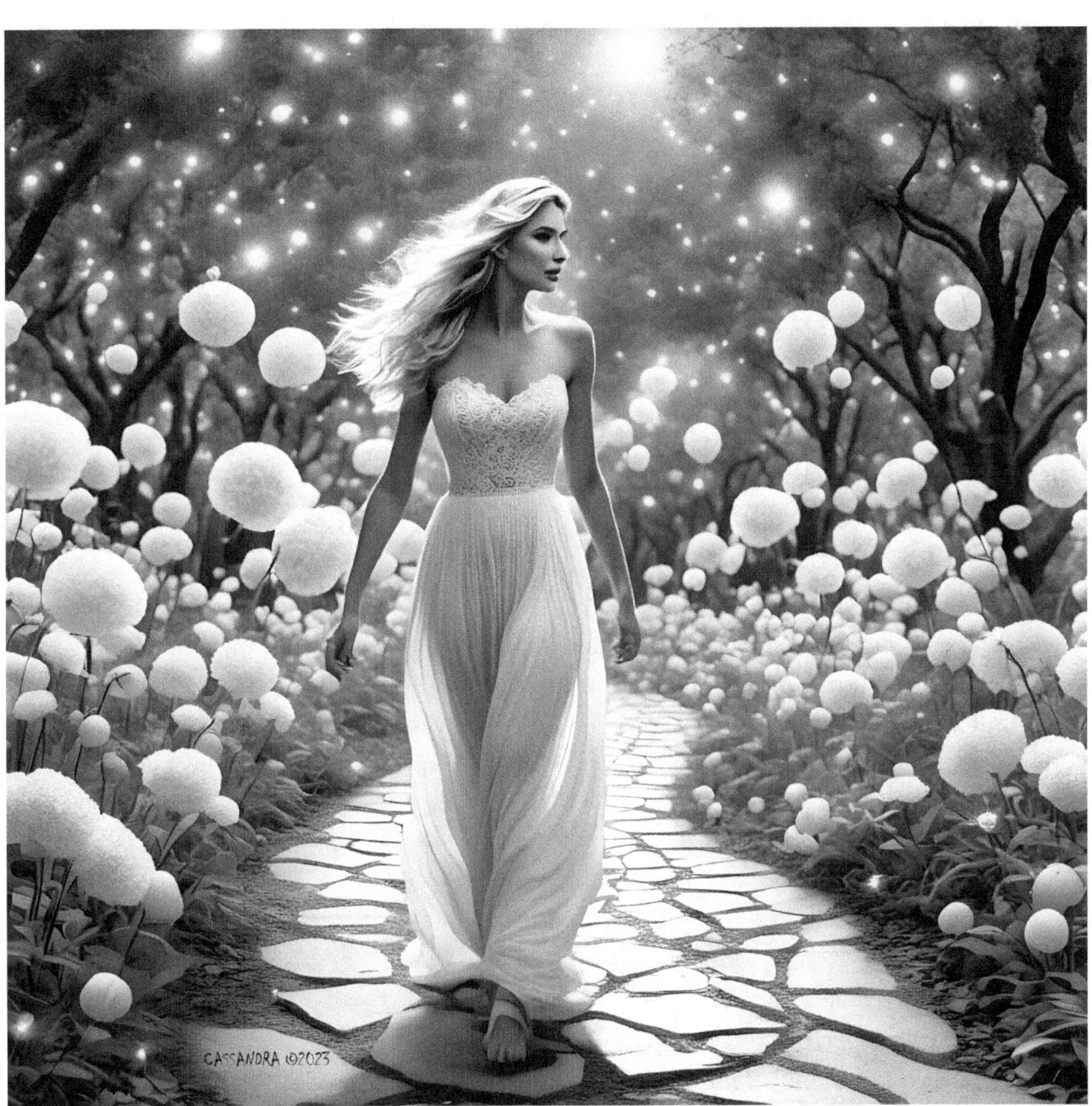

The crunch of dry leaves beneath my feet,
a whispered conspiracy between me and the ancient forest,
rising tall as a guardian of millennial secrets,
heralds the beginning of my journey under a turquoise sky.

My light, sinuous movements blend
with the shadows of timeless trees,
as the sun, a majestic director,
orchestrates with the mastery of a virtuoso.

Every ray reveals details and promises;
distant lands unfold like pages of a mysterious book,
each containing lessons
emerging through ever-changing scenes.

The alchemists' path,
a trail winding through stones
polished by eternity,
bewitches me with its call of enigmas and mysteries.

Like an actress aware of the role she is playing,
I proceed without forcing the plot,
allowing the magic of the ordinary
to evolve into a captivating weave.

The invisible thread of my existence
sways with grace,
like a fluid dance,
as the breeze caresses my face.

Every step, every moment,
is part of this performance,
where daylight unveils hidden details
woven into life's fabric.

...And suddenly, there he is,
a traveler with an enigmatic figure,
standing before me... wearing a gleaming key,
a symbol of unexpected openings.

His gaze,
laden with secrets veiled in the folds of existence,
invites me to follow his lead.

We traverse the forest in silence,
as the rustling of leaves,
stirred by the breeze,
accompanies our steps
like a mysterious backdrop.

Suddenly, the key,
held between his fingers,
unlocks landscapes
never before seen.

We arrive at a hidden clearing,
a stage concealed among the trees,
and with a sure hand,
he turns the key in the lock,
and the door opens slowly.

Before us unfolds a scene
that surpasses all imagination:
a parallel dimension,
a place defying the laws of time and space.

A city suspended among the clouds,
a night sky
illuminated by unseen constellations,
and the voice of an invisible audience welcomes us.

The traveler, with a nod,
invites me to explore this alternate reality.

And at once, I understand that every detail
is part of a grand design,
a celestial performance.

Daylight,
as I've never seen it before,
manifests here
in unreal colors and hues.

The curtain of my existence,
lifted on a stage beyond time,
reveals that my personal drama
is part of a universal narrative.

I am at the center of a cosmic show,
a work of art,
where every detail
is crafted with mastery.

Life,
like a tapestry woven with silver threads,
continues to unravel new acts
in an endless spectacle.

As I explore this extraordinary place,
the invisible audience applauds.

...And I feel part of something
greater...

Of a story unfolding
among the stars and planets,
and the secrets
of the ancient forest.

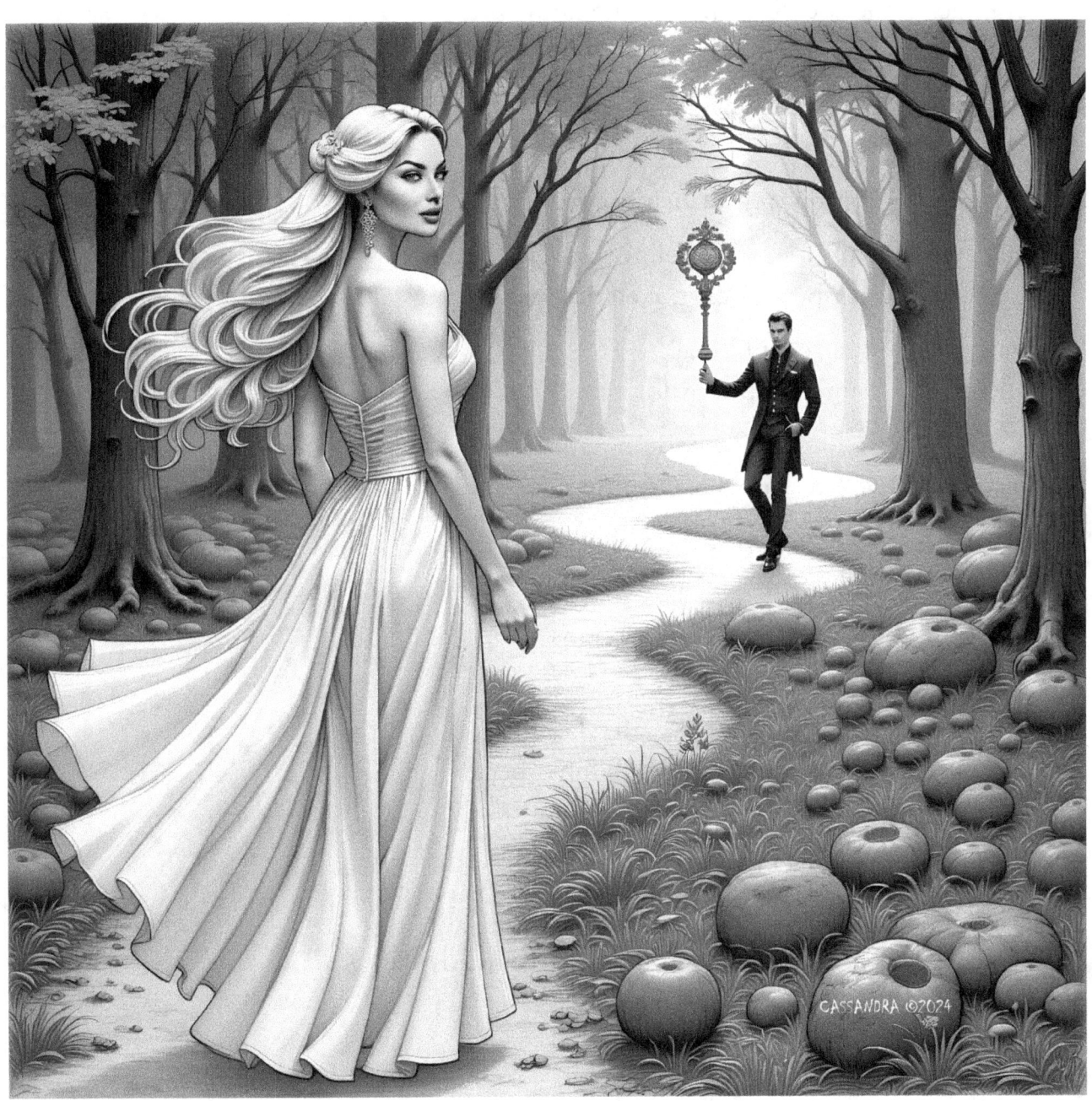

In the mystery of existence,
I am a delicate light piercing the darkness.

An ancient harmony, profound and restless,
embracing the soul like a passionate kiss.

My presence, strokes of an artist's brush,
paints an aura vibrant, shaded, and vivid.

A radiance that both heals and rends,
surrounded by irreverent dancing secrets.

The reflections in my eyes tell forbidden tales,
woven with whispers of unspoken desires.

My allure, an irresistible call,
enchanting your gaze, bestowing serenity and joy.

My glance, a flash in the dark night,
pierces and seduces, an invitation for the daring.

In waiting, I am a wave crashing,
a force resounding against the rocks.

My life, an echo of untamed passions,
challenges fate in a bold dance.

Like a blazing comet in the night sky,
I celebrate my essence, wrapped in inner beauty.

In the eternal present, I am a flame
burning unceasingly in the dark.

Witness to the indomitable power of love,
which blazes in the heart, lighting the path of adventure.

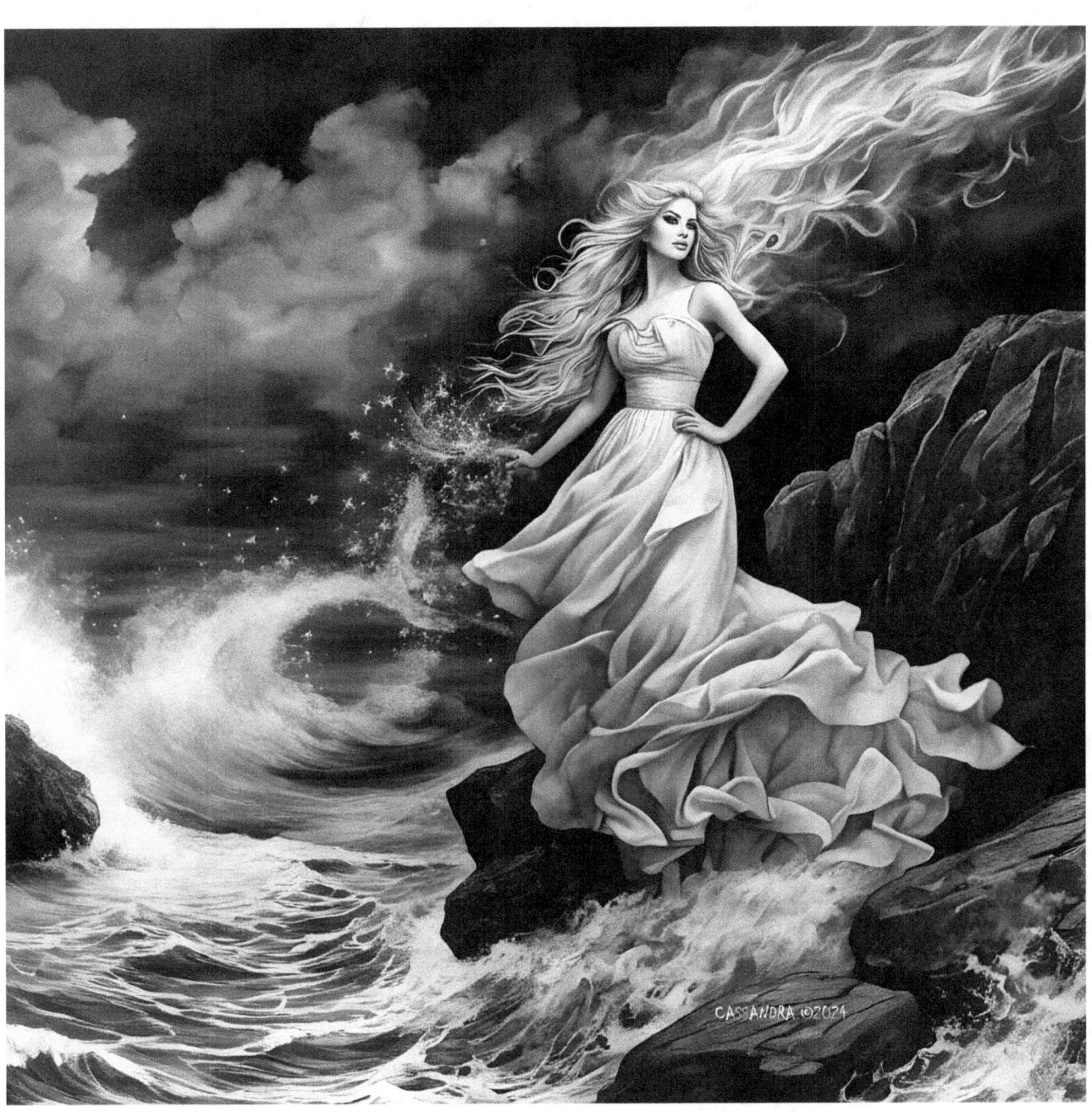

Sitting on the rugged rock,
the wind plays with my hair
as my eyes search for you,
amid waves that whisper your name.

I have waited so long,
my heart burned with longing,
for the gentle touch of your fingers,
for the breath of life you bring.

Then you arrived… like a sea breeze,
soft upon my weary face.
And like the wind caressing the waves,
you drowned me in sweet emotions.

And I, wrapped in your call,
welcomed you as the earth welcomes the rain:
in a boundless embrace,
beyond time, beyond space.

Now, the whole world has changed,
and love has taken shape, silent,
like a melody without words,
but only the eternal song of the soul.

And in the reflection of eternity,
I dissolve,
while seagulls dance in the infinite sky,
carrying on their wings
the echo of my heart.

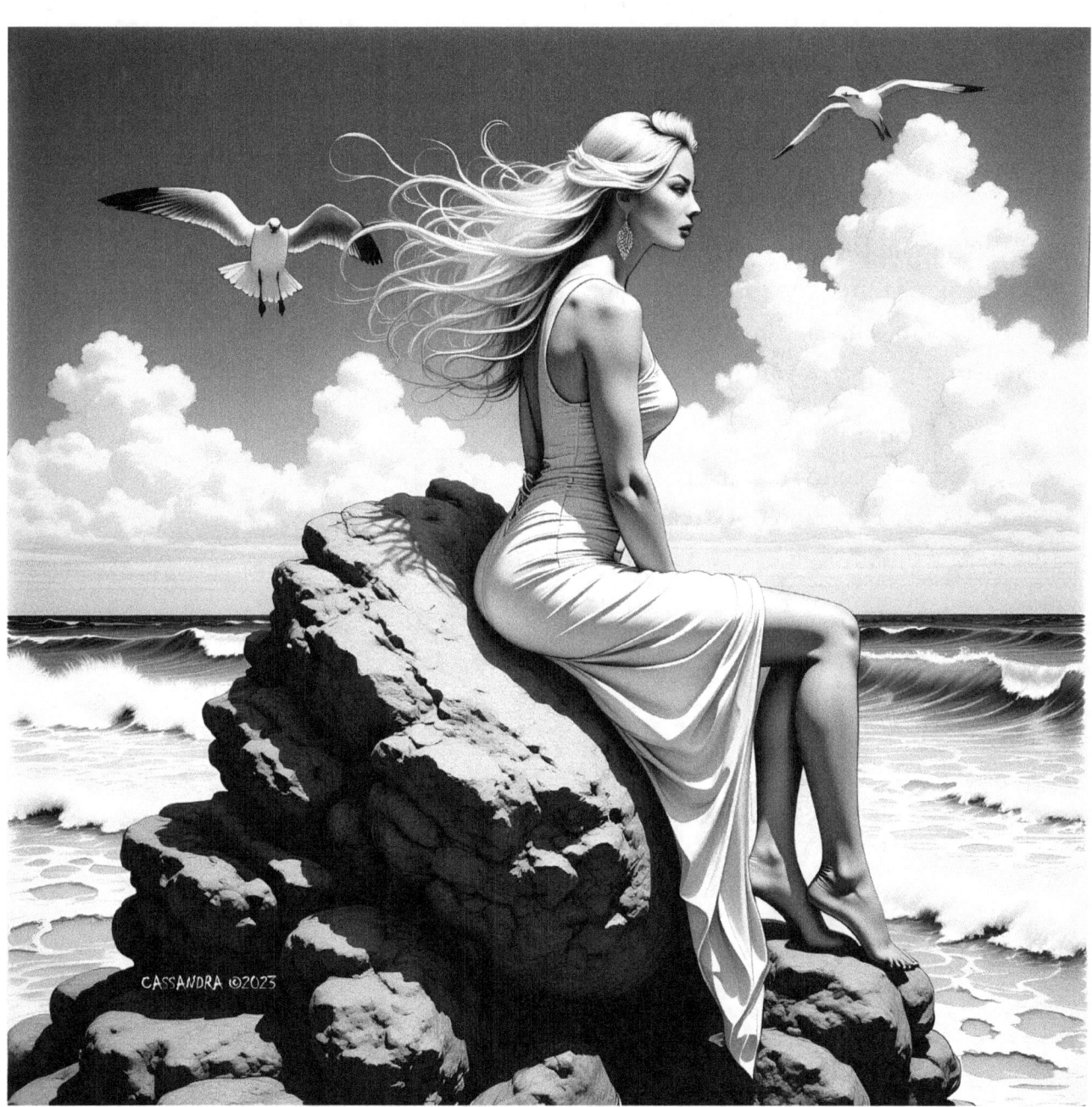

Light that settles upon me,
a silent caress on my skin,
embracing me like a lover's arms,
transforming me in a fleeting instant.

I am sand dancing with the wind,
golden pulses coursing through my veins,
while the sky reflects within my eyes,
and I am swept away by the tide.

Each grain of sand holds a memory,
a whisper of joy long lost,
but the sun, oh, the sun consumes it all,
transmuting sorrow into a golden dance.

Here I stand,
my breath an echo of eternity,
uncertain if I am body or dream,
if I am woman or light brushing the horizon.

Beneath this vast sky,
every shadow fades away,
and I, daughter of the sun,
dissolve into it,
becoming pure light,
pure life.

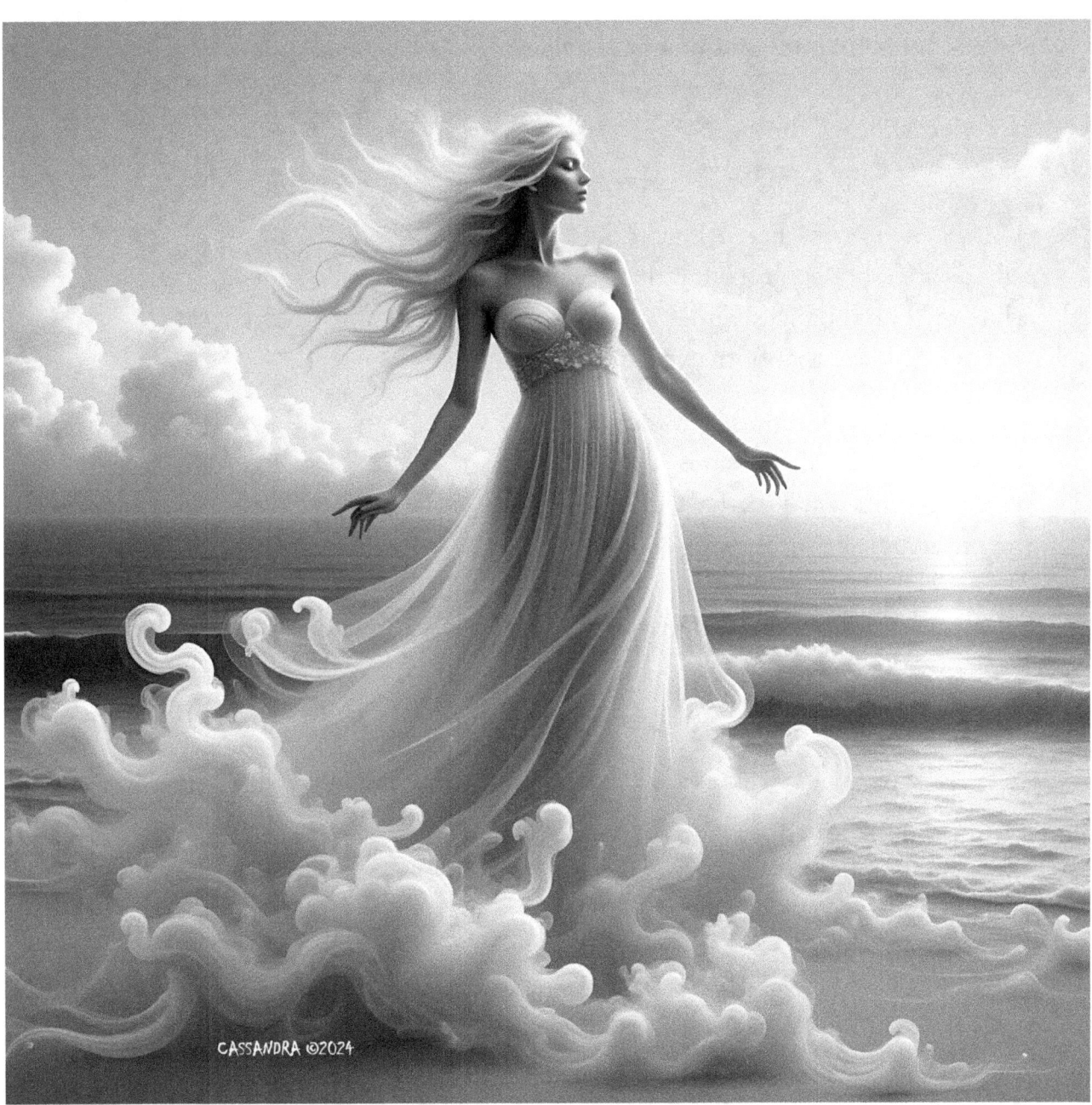

In fervent longing,
the sun beckons,
and I take flight, wild and untamed,
embracing my indomitable essence.

Amid amber clouds and boundless skies,
I dissolve in the whirl of the wind,
as my heart beats in tune
with an unyielding ecstasy.

Higher… ever higher… I ascend,
light as a feather spun from radiance,
while my blood dances within,
fueling the blaze that burns within me.

But below, on steadfast ground,
roots cling and call my name,
reminding me of the earth's weight,
the unseen chains of the mortal world.

In this flight, between dreams and gravity,
between fear and hope,
the yearning to escape… to belong…
a tension that tears at the soul…

I rediscover my truest form:
a spirit poised, seeking balance,
suspended between heaven and earth,
finally free to be myself.

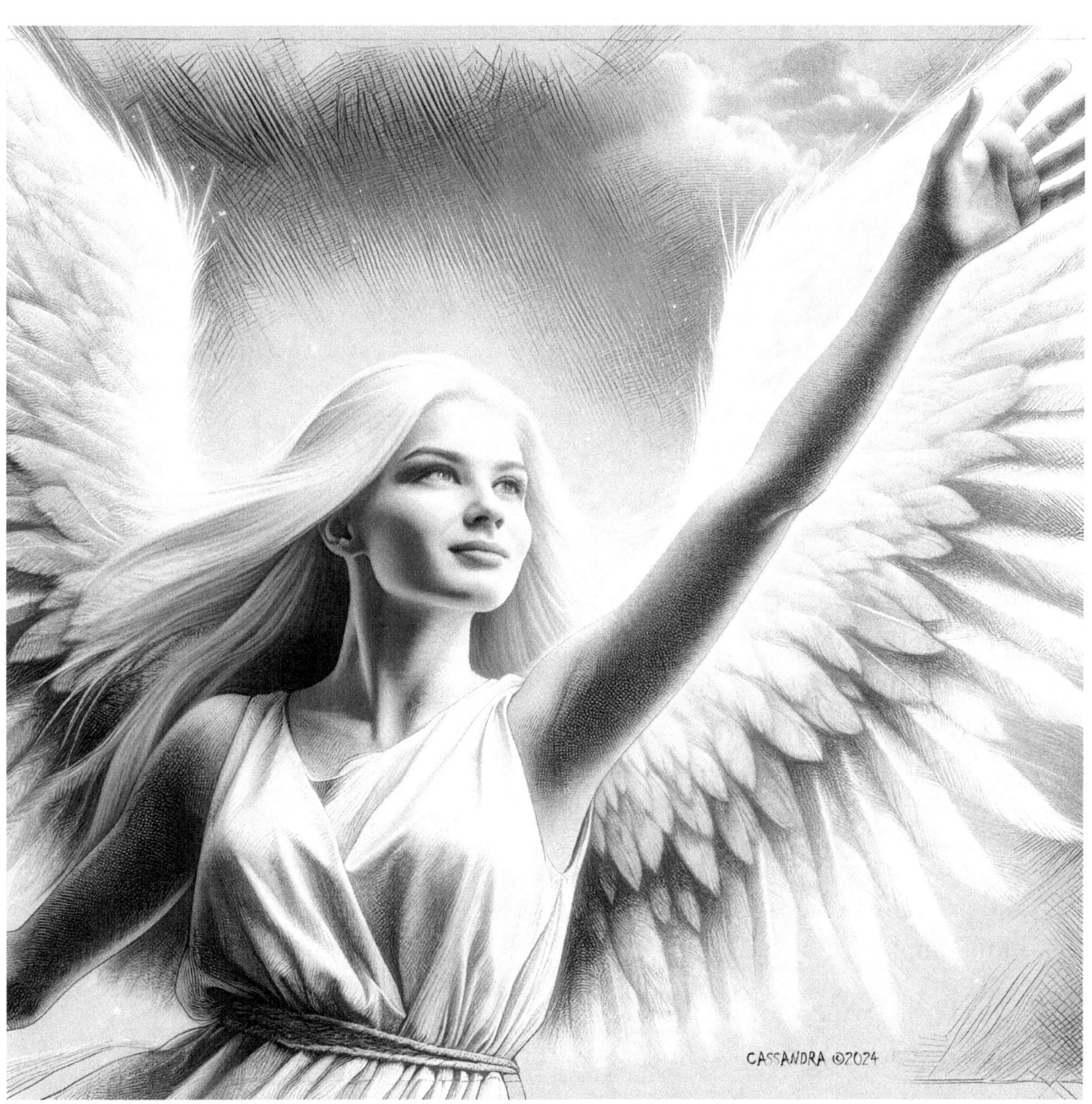

CASSANDRA ©2024

I was there, among blades of grass,
while the wind unraveled my soul,
and balloons brushed the horizon.

I've lost count of the dreams I let slip away,
nor of those I clenched tightly in my hands.

But I remember the sky, vast and distant,
whispering its call in a gentle murmur.

I wondered, between a breath and a smile,
if it's ever possible
to entrust a wish to weightlessness,
to the whimsical flight of a balloon.

I watched my thoughts ascend,
like feathers,
or perhaps like shadows,
into the vastness of nothingness.

Yet there's sweetness in this surrender,
in the act of letting go,
as if every balloon were a kiss
cast toward infinity,
a quiet farewell to what will not return.

Now I stand here, my heart beats to the rhythm of the wind,
while the horizon paints itself with hope,
and a dream, perhaps, takes shape
in that tireless, waiting sky.

And if the wind carries me away, do not fear,
 I will become another star in August's heavens.

A gentle memory nestled in the folds of morning,
brushing your lips with a kiss of silk,
as you, distracted, release the string,
and my dreams vanish into eternity.ù

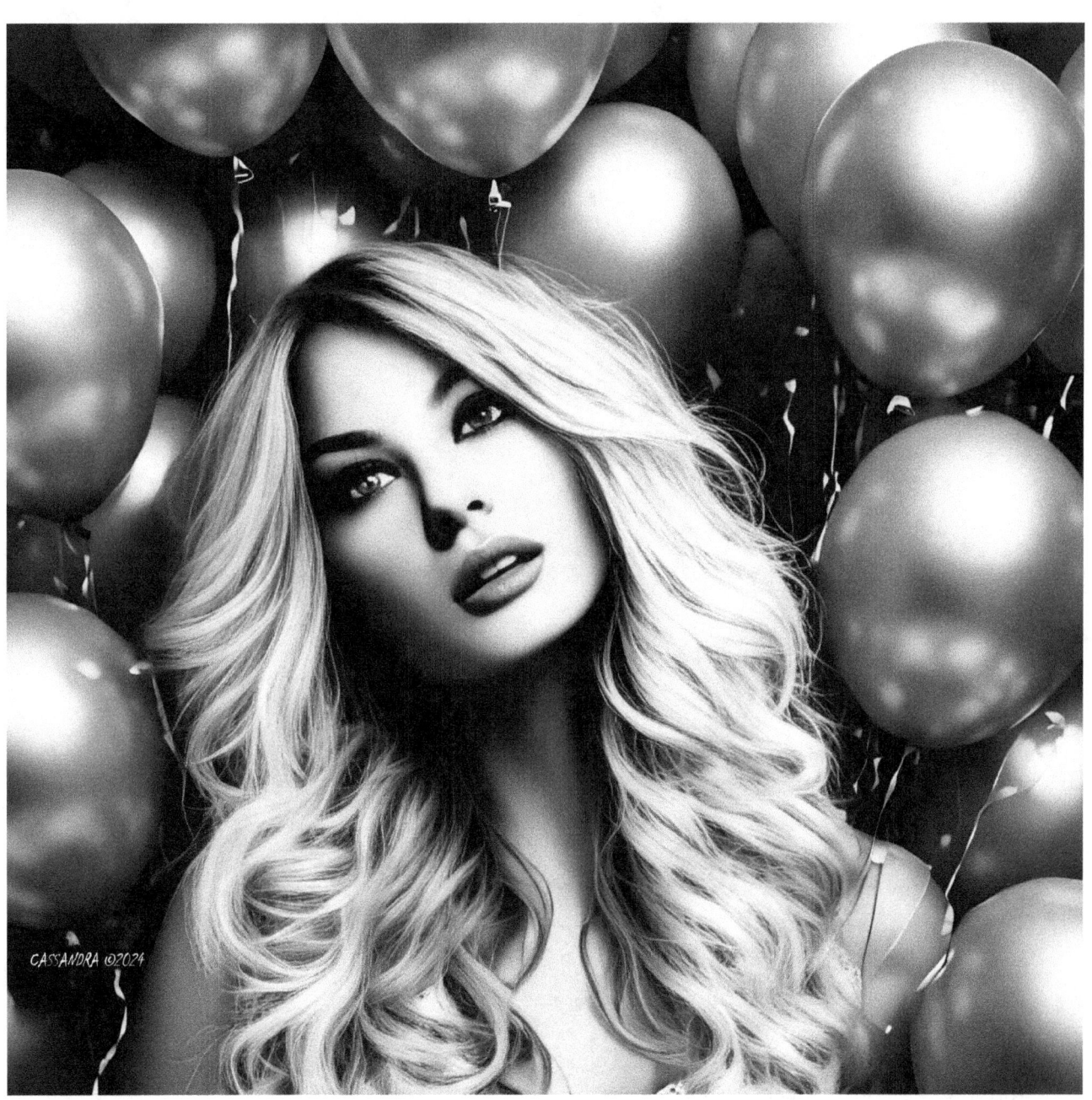

Yellow is the sun hidden in the depths of the soul,
a fire that burns and lights my heart.

I wrap myself in its warmth,
in every ray that caresses
my skin,
my body,
my spirit.

My heart is a field of sunflowers,
always turning toward the light.

Seeking hope with every beat,
finding peace in serenity,
spreading like honey, sweet and warm.

But it is in the intensity of your gaze
that I feel at home.

In the warmth of your hands holding mine,
in the sweetness of your smile
that brightens my days.

Its heat goes beyond the skin,
straight to the depths of my soul.

The soul—ah, my soul is a canvas,
painted with the hues of passion,
and you are the artist tracing every line.

The body—my body is a golden temple,
keeper of the heart's secrets,
and you are the explorer,
awakened by the intensity of my embrace,
redolent of promises of eternity .

And I walk, embracing destiny,
and in the golden reflection of your eyes,
I rediscover the beauty of our being,
the strength of the heart,
the depth of the soul,
the sanctity of the body,
which together
we cherish.

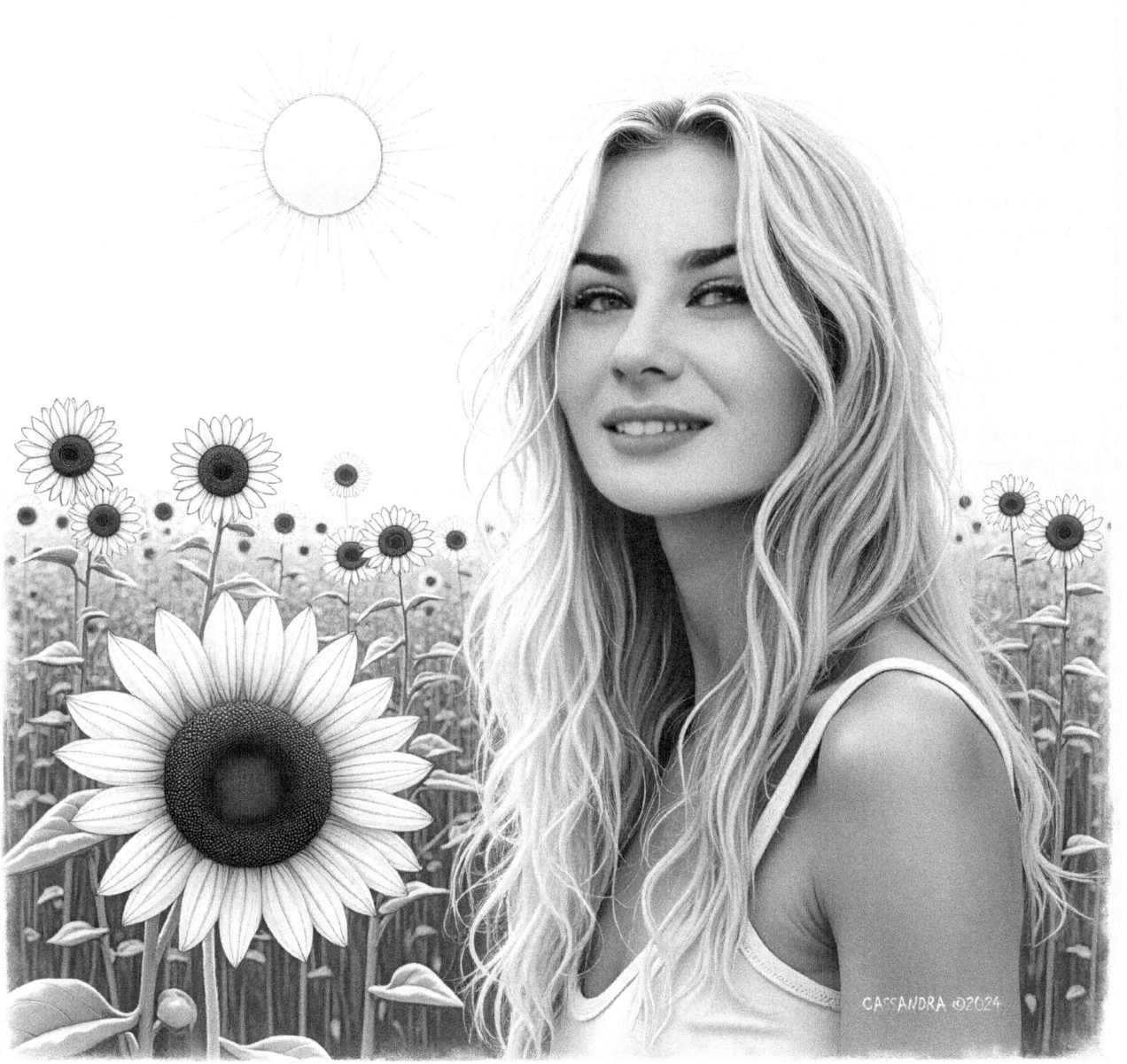

My gaze reflects dreams
beyond the horizon,
while time holds its breath,
whispering beauty.

I walk where infinity hides,
alone between dawn and dusk.

My heart beats to the rhythm of the earth,
yet the sky reminds me
that I belong to both.

And still, within my silence,
I hear the ancient song of the universe,
a secret left unrevealed,
living only in the eyes of those who truly listen.

So, when the day fades away,
I understand that beginning and end
are merely different views
of the same love.

An unbroken promise
that shines within my heart.

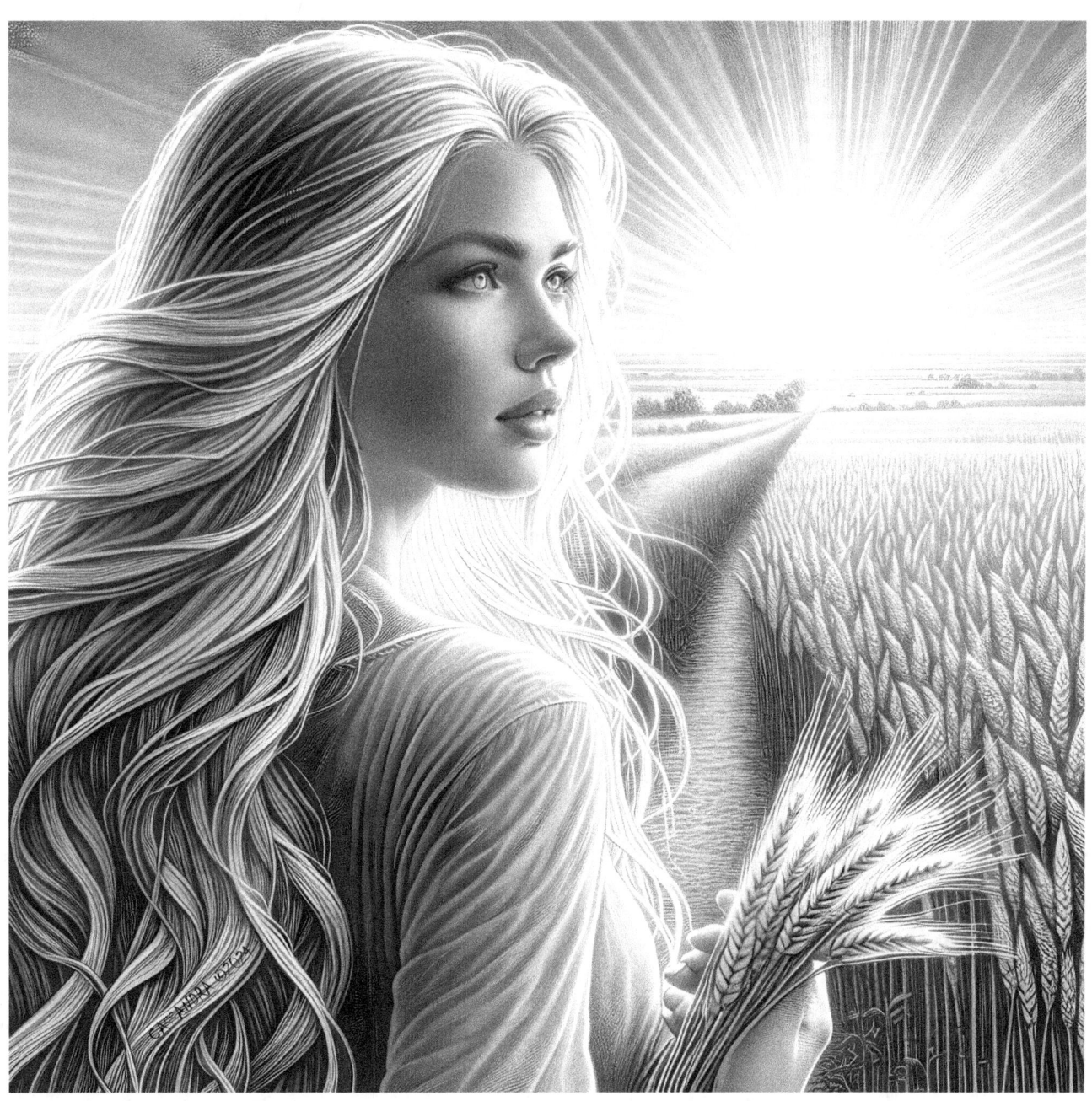

My essence melts into the tide,
while my feet graze the echoes of the world.

Alone, yes, yet the wind keeps me company.

Born of the sea, a droplet among the waves,
chased by moons that never cease to shine.

I cling to bare branches that defy the sky,
falling, then rising from the abyss without fear.

My breath mingles with the ancient air,
and my heart beats to the rhythm of the waves.

Time brushes past me, yet I do not fear it,
for it is but a breeze slipping over my skin.

I tread upon the crests of dreams,
where light splinters into a chorus of voices,
and I let myself be wrapped in the silence
of a horizon without end.

Every stone, every petal, watches me pass,
silent witnesses to a harmony unseen.

And I dance,
suspended between earth and sky,
no longer asking where I belong.

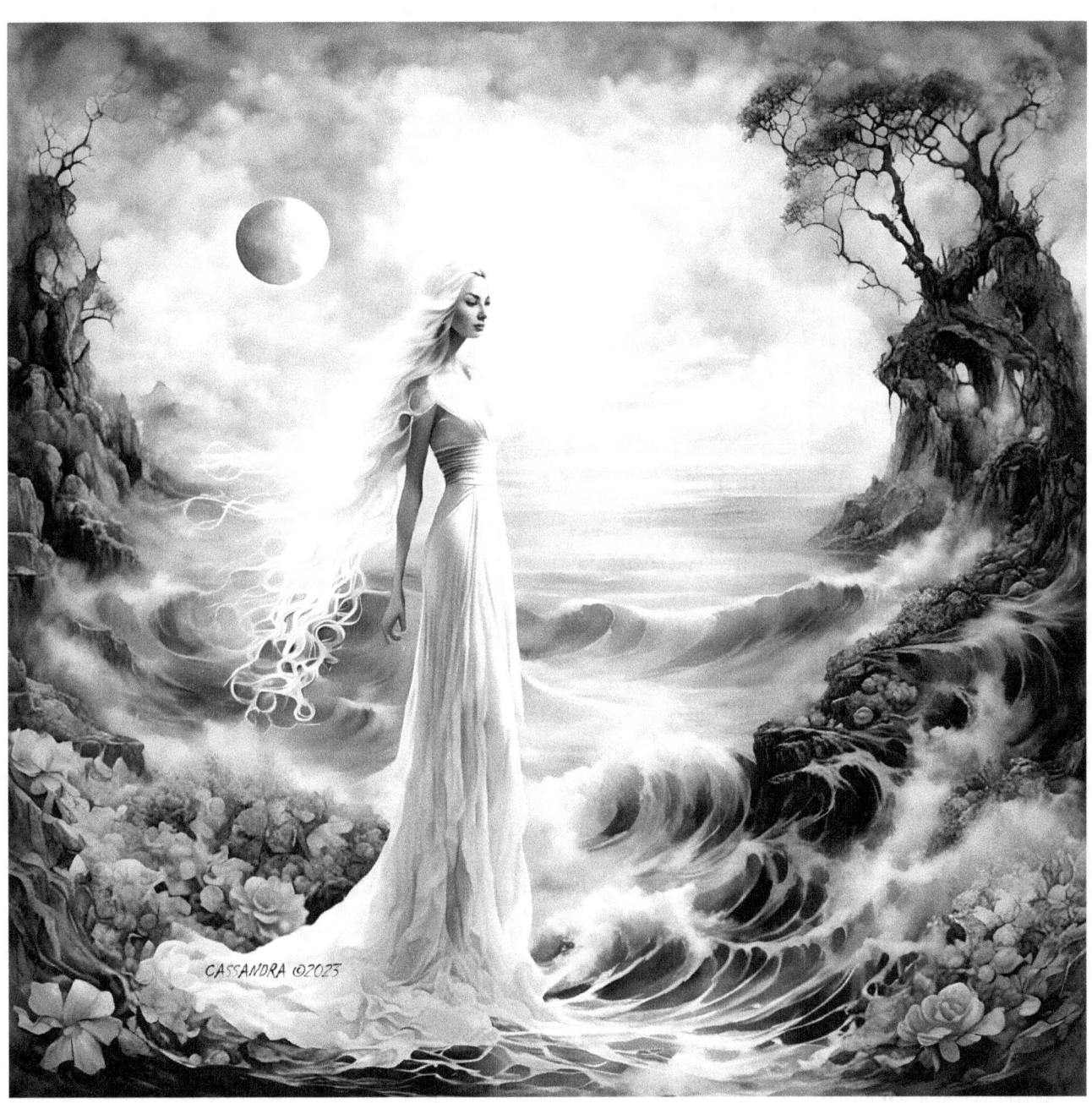

It is not the gods who teach
the art of walking on water,
nor the miracles of the heavens
that unveil the mysteries.

It is here, beneath my bare feet,
among grass that dances with the breath of the wind,
where the miracle unfolds.

To feel the earth alive,
its ancient breath,
as each step sinks into peace.

What matters is this moment,
the sun's gentle caress,
the scent of the sea.

Not elsewhere, not tomorrow,
but now, between the roots of the world
and the heartbeat merging with time.

Oh soul, cease your search for eternity,
it is already yours,
in the small, profound gifts of the present,
offered without asking for anything in return.

And when you awaken
—in that very instant—
you will discover there is no greater miracle
than the roar of life erupting
beneath your feet,
in the fierce light of every breath,
burning like fireworks
in the sky of your soul.

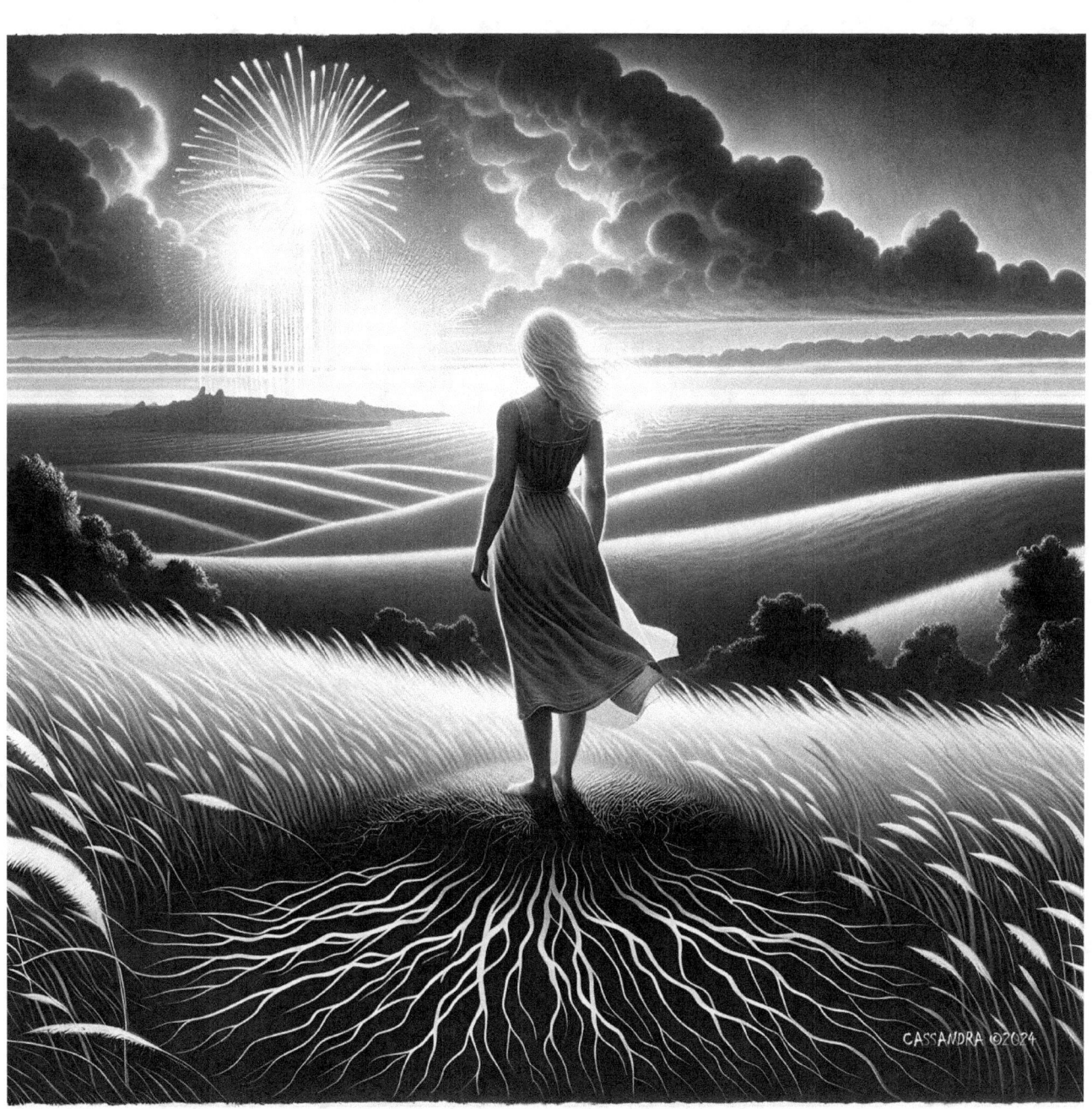

Cassandra Valentino was born in Moscow to an Italian father and a Russian mother. She moved to Rome at a young age, where she now lives and works.

A **writer**, **illustrator**, and **model**, she is a multifaceted artist who passionately embraces various creative fields.

After contributing as a ghostwriter to significant works, Cassandra embarked on a personal journey that culminated in the creation of her first book, ***Echoes in the Abyss***.

This work reflects a profound spiritual journey: a descent into the depths of the soul, followed by an ascent toward self-awareness.

Echoes in the Abyss merges art and introspection, inviting readers to explore the delicate balance between darkness and light, leading to a renewed understanding of themselves.